In assocation with...The Yuvraj Singh Liposuction Clinic

THE ALTERNATIVE CRICKET
ALMANACK
2011

From the Editor...

Simply, cricket is a game to love, cherish and enjoy.

This book was born out of a frustration at being force-fed corporate drivel on the airwaves, and turgid prose on the web and in print. As such, we have gathered a crack team of writers sharing the same ethos.

There is no watershed in our book, which includes frequent outbursts of profanity. If we offend your sensibilities, there's always Harry Potter.

We hope you enjoy.

Nishant Joshi

Sub–editors:

Lizzy Ammon

Half–Tracker

Subash Jayaraman

Staff writers:

Antony Chettupuzha

Legsidefilth

Adrian McGruther

Paul Sculpher

Stuart Millson

Sana Kazmi

Robert Hicks

Jarrod Kimber

Daniel Norcross

Lucy Sweetman

Leslie Knott

Aram Margarian

Timothy Bunting

The Cricket Widow

Back cover photo by Sarah Ansell – sarahcanterbury.com

If you enjoy our articles, please feel free to drop us an email if you would like to solicit any of our writers. We don't mind whoring ourselves out.

Email: home@thealternativecricketalmanack.com

www.TheAlternativeCricketAlmanack.com

Twitter.com/TheAltAlmanack

Disclaimer: No offence is intended, apart from where we reference the Akmal brothers.

Referring From the Grave

News article:

There is now photographic proof that when Don Bradman was bowled in his last Test innings for a duck, the bowler had bowled a no-ball. The bowler, name not provided, had stepped over the bowling crease line which at that time was a back foot no-ball, meaning that Bradman could not have been given out. In the photo, which has been found at an English charity shop, it is obvious that the umpire is not watching the line and is instead looking at Bradman.

Had Bradman made four more runs, he would have ended with a batting average of 100.0.

Centennial Park Cemetery, **Adelaide**.

The cemetery is quiet, no emo kids having sex in graveyards tonight. Then, there is a quiet scratching noise in the graveyard. Like a bird gnawing at something inside a tree. The noise continues to get louder and more frenzied. A strong, old hand breaks the turf on a grave. The hand struggles to get any grip, but slowly and surely, a corpse makes its way out of the grave, dressed in a suit and with a green cap on its head.

The old corpse is still well-preserved and is quick on its feet, as it makes its way to a service station and lines up behind a bunch of loud youths. They get some money out, and then bump into the old corpse, calling him 'grandpa' as they walk past him. They walk away, not knowing that he has stolen their wallets. Next, the old corpse tells the service station attendant that the toilet is broken, and when the attendant leaves to fix the toilet, the old corpse slips behind the counter in an unorthodox manner and steals a few grand before disappearing into the night.

ICC headquarters, Dubai.

The old corpse arrives at the reception desk of the ICC. Wearing a new suit, the same green cap, and with a leather briefcase.

"Excuse me young lady, I am here to register a referral."

"A referral for what?"

"For an umpiring decision."

"Oh, well sorry, they can only be done on the ground, by a batsman or captain."

"I understand, but at the time I played, the referral system was not active, and I would like to register it now. The bowler who got me out had bowled an illegitimate ball so it means I should not given out and my record should be changed. I have a photo, and…"

"Sorry, but we can't do that."

"Can I speak to whoever is in charge of the ICC?"

"None of them are in Dubai at the moment."

"Oh, that is annoying. Is there anything you can do for me?"

"I'm afraid not, the ICC cannot refer decisions from Test matches that have ended, you need to refer it within a brief period of time on the field."

"That is a shame, I came all this way. Never mind, it isn't your fault. Can I use your bathroom?"

The receptionist shows him where it is. The old corpse does his business and waits for others to leave. He then fiddles in his leather briefcase for a moment, and then leaves it on the ground.

The old corpse gets back into his rental car, and drives away. Behind him is a tremendous explosion. He doesn't react to it at all and just pushes a CD into the player.

> *"Who is it that all Australia raves about?*
>
> *Who has won our very highest praise?*
>
> *Now is it Amy Johnson, or little Mickey Mouse?*
>
> *No! it's just a country lad who's bringing down the house…"*

Jarrod Kimber is the critically ignored, warped mind behind cricketwithballs.com. Now in 3D.

Seven Things I Hate About Cricket

Lalit Modi

Better known to users of Twitter as *@LalitKModi*, I have always appreciated the man's business acumen from a distance. However, his self-aggrandisation has reached Allen 'Ponzi? What Ponzi?' Stanford proportions. Asking cameras to pan to him at every spare moment, Modi is the former ringleader of his IPL circus, and he wants us all to know about it. It's not that we don't appreciate the IPL; it's that we never appreciated the notion that it was run exclusively by a money-hungry tyrant.

After christening himself 'The Commissioner', you could be forgiven for thinking that Modi was an evil character in his own wrestling pantomime. Crucially, by ensuring that he always received the lion's share of camera time, Modi robbed us of a valuable opportunity to leer at Shilpa Shetty, who is the sole reason to ever watch a Rajasthan Royals game. The entire cricket world was turned upside down when Modi was permanently suspended due to 'financial irregularities'; unjustly, if you were to believe the good man's Twitter page.

With a seemingly unquenchable desire to become a martyr, Lalit K. Modi is now undergoing proceedings to legally change his name to Martin Lalit King.

Hate Factor: 6/10

Grass

It's the height of summer. Your village Sunday 3rd XI is relying on you to hold onto a top-edged skier. You're stationed at fine leg, even though you have spent the whole innings moaning about how you're athletic enough to field at cover point.

You run round, get in position, cup your hands 'Aussie style', but to your horror, your nose starts to itch. Your eyes start to run. Your face starts to contort, and your eyes are blinded by the sun as you stare straight up into the clear blue sky.

And then it comes: The Sneeze.

Not just one; not two; but three machine-gun sneezes, as a red missile plummets towards your head, at unimaginable speed.

You blink.

When you open your eyes a mere millisecond later, you are dazed, and your head feels like you've spent the night playing Pub Golf with Andrew Symonds. Your teammates are staring daggers; in half-teapot unison you could be forgiven for thinking that the batsman had just tackled a streaker on the field of play. You feel mucus all across your face, but you can't see for shit through your puffy eyes. Pollen-stained tears drip down your face, and act to disguise their companion, less stinging tears from your imminent emotional scars. You dropped a regulation top-edge and you

10

want the whole world to swallow you up.

Yes, dear readers: I have hayfever, and as a result of this, I now suffer from frightening deja vu moments every time Shahid Afridi is at the crease.

Hate Factor: 8/10

Rudi Koertzen

The man reminds me of a traffic warden. Koertzen is an irritating jobsworth who seems to be convinced in his own self-importance. This man made a living out of making wrong decisions, and yet was on an impressive salary, for a job which, as cricket die-hards, we would happily do free of charge.

His 'finger of death' was indicative of his own uncertainty, and thanks to the introduction of HawkEye, we were finally backed up by solid evidence in our assertions that Koertzen was out to destroy the careers of emerging batsmen. If it wasn't for his grating personality and logic-defying explanations of his decisions, I could happily dismiss Rudi as just another incompetent umpire. However, as he seemed to be so intent on ruining the game which we so love, he must go down as an all-time enemy of the game.

When he retired in 2010, cricket fans rejoiced. But spare a thought for the effigy-makers, and for South African bowlers,

11

whose stock plummeted in the immediate aftermath of Koertzen's retirement.

Hate Factor: 10/10

The 'middle overs' in ODI's

Overs 0–15 and 40–50 are always entertaining enough to keep our attention. This is the time where the Sehwags and Gayles mix it up with the Iqbals and McCullums. These are the players we tune in for. We watch limited overs cricket for the flamboyance of Tendulkar; not the stodgy accumulation of Kallis. The middle overs are riddled with mundane singles and commentators complimenting the batsmen who are adept at 'milking' the bowling for exactly six singles per over.

Although as a cricket lover, I appreciate a Collingwood nurdle into midwicket as much as the next person, watching three of these every over for the best part of two hours is mind-numbingly monotonous. The middle overs makes us lose appreciation for cricket altogether, as we are bored into submission by 'good running', 'building a partnership', and Danny Morrison's inane descriptions of how "ladies' clothes in Jaipur aren't as colourful as they are in Rajasthan, are they Ravi?"

Hate Factor: 7/10

Lily Allen

Her pretending to like cricket in 2009 ruined my Ashes. I was prepared for rain, thunder and bad light; but not for Lily Allen. Her infamous Test Match Special interview with a lovestruck Jonathan Agnew was very much a case of the high school cheerleader toying with the hapless geek, and it would have been cruel had it not been such an overt PR exercise. I have a lot of respect for Lily Allen the singer, although I can't quite relate to her music directly. For example, when she proffers: "I spent ages giving head" in her single 'It's not fair', Lily tries to relate an interesting dilemma to us, to which I can only offer my uneasy sympathy.

Hate Factor: 8/10

Australian cricketers who start conversations with "Look mate" or "Awww mate"

'Nuff said.

Hate Factor: 6/10

Mark Nicholas

When charm becomes smarm. Nicholas is a commentator who is single-handedly attempting to destroy the very fabric of cricket as we know it. I can totally appreciate the man as a handsome, seemingly never-ageing being, with a voice so smooth that he should be sponsoring Lurpak. I wholly appreciate and even occasionally indulge in the 21st century practice of 'guy love', but Mark Nicholas takes it to embarrassing new levels. If he was chatting in a bar with his everlong '*plat du jour*' Michael Clarke, one's mind would naturally wander to which of the couple prefers to be the big spoon.

Many heartily agree with the assertion that Nicholas is a 'housewives' favourite', but I counter this common myth by asking you: how many housewives watch cricket? I cannot correlate housewives sighing over Mark Nicholas with men watching a Sky Sports News just to ogle Georgie Thompson. His insistence on shamelessly plugging sponsors at the most inappropriate times has also worn me down: "And he's got a hat-trick to seal the match! Let's see what Betfair Richie makes of all this! Lara Bingle is a slut!"

Nicholas seems to be pleasuring the Channel 9 sponsors at every opportunity, to the extent that he might as well be having $1 bills stuffed down his glittery G-string. Nobody forced corporate dick down your throat, Mark, but your orgies of ignorance with pillow-pals Ian Healy and Mark Taylor make me want to vomit like never before.

It is totally plausible that Nicholas' life is boiling down to one moment: Michael Clarke's wedding. Having been shunned as best man, he will infiltrate the gathering, waiting to pounce when the words "Does anybody have any objections?" are uttered.

14

There, he will throw a hissyfit for the ages, before eventually settling for his second-choice, Shane Watson.

Hate Factor: If Robert Mugabe had an evil twin, his name would be Mark Nicholas.

Born in London, Nishant Joshi is a medical student in the Czech Republic with a passion for writing and his guitar. He is a social philanthropist, without the money.

Afghan Cricket: Beyond the Boundary

By purchasing this book – assuming that you're not freeloading off us in a bookshop – you will be supporting the Afghan Youth Cricket Support Organisation via The Alternative Cricket Scholarship Fund. **Leslie Knott** has played an integral part in setting up and supporting the AYCSO, and gives us insight into what it's like to be involved in Afghan cricket...

The AYCSO was founded by former Afghan national cricket captain Raees Ahmadzai. Although he had been working with grassroots cricket development in an informal way for years, it was in 2009 that he registered an NGO: the Afghan Youth Cricket Support Organization. Projects before registration included 'Hit Polio for a Six', which trained children in cricket skills in unstable regions of Afghanistan, while also educating about polio.

Since 2009, the AYCSO has formally trained over 800 children, both boys and girls. Working in some of the most remote, insecure provinces where children rarely have access to sport, the AYCSO is committed to providing an alternative to war and conflict. By introducing children to cricket, it provides much needed activity and encourages confidence building and cooperation.

Players between the ages of 6 and 24 have participated in the camps, and come from a variety of backgrounds. Some children have cricketing experience, while others have never picked up a bat or ball. The camps take place once a month and we are currently raising funds in order to build an Academy of Excellence in Kabul, where we can hold week-long cricket camps.

Since the recent success of the Afghan national team, there has been a meteoric rise in interest in the sport. However, the biggest obstacle facing us is working with girls. Due to the cultural sensitivity and social stigmas in Afghanistan, it has been a monumental struggle to incorporate training for girls. Our experience shows that men do support girls playing cricket, as long as they adhere to the Islamic way of playing sport. Even the Taliban don't have a problem with cricket – when the national team qualified for the ICC World Twenty20 in Dubai, the Taliban fired RPG's in celebration! In spite of this, opportunities for Afghan girls to play any sort of sport are painfully limited.

It is the mission of the AYCSO to set up an Academy of Excellence in Kabul, where children can come from the provinces to take part in high quality cricket training. Currently, we are partially funded through UNICEF and Afghan Connection, an NGO which builds schools and cricket pitches.

A typical day would consist of exercise, batting and bowling practice, as well as theory about rules of the game, and building confidence among the participants. Meals would be rice, meat and salad – the daily Afghan staple. The Afghan team had atrocious eating habits when they won their maiden international tournament in Jersey, with McDonald's and KFC being binge favourites!

At present, we have no facilities to speak of. We are in dire need of nets, bowling machines, and basic equipment such as bats and pads. Currently, we are training on dusty concrete slabs and patchy grass – not exactly conducive to developing talent, of which there is plenty on display.

We need to raise $45,000 in order to build facilities that have professional equipment such as nets and bowling machines.

The money raised would help pay for children who have qualified for the camp, enabling them to travel from the provinces, as well as paying for food and accommodation. Money collected from The Alternative Cricket Scholarship Fund will help pay for children from the provinces to attend the week-long camps, and we will accommodate the children in hostels at the Olympic Committee, which is right beside the proposed cricket academy.

Even with bombs bursting in the distance, cricket is a fortifying sport which has an admirable record of bringing people together. The advantages of children playing cricket should be obvious to anybody who has played the sport, at any level.

The success of the Afghan national team has proven that there is awesome raw talent, but for it to thrive, we must keep introducing youngsters to the game and enabling them to develop their natural abilities. Moreover, a successful national sports team would be a beacon of hope for a nation ravaged by war.

By contributing to our scholarship fund, you could be helping to unearth the next Afridi or Tendulkar, and as such, your support is greatly appreciated.

Leslie Knott is a Canadian freelance filmmaker and photographer who didn't know what a wicket was when she started filming the Afghan cricket team in May 2008. After spending two years following the team on their World Cup journey, she not only started to enjoy cricket, but she also joined forces with Raees Ahmadzai to start the AYCSO.

We Need to STFU About KP

"Yep.. Done for rest of summer!! Man of the World Cup T20 and dropped from the T20 side too.. Its a fuck up!! Surrey have signed me for l ..."

Kevin Pietersen, @kevinpp24 on Twitter, on his exclusion from the England ODI and T20 squads, Tuesday, 31st August 2010.

"He has a security guard either side of him! It's ridiculous! What do you need a security guard coming down the steps for?" So shrieked Michael Atherton, with barely concealed disbelief and a hint of gleeful scorn as Kevin Pietersen took the field for Surrey atThe Oval, the day after England's most talented batsman let slip on Twitter – before hastily deleting it a few minutes later – that the England selectors had dropped him for the forthcoming T20 and ODI matches against Pakistan.

Kevin Pietersen pisses off a lot of people. Arrogant. Plays for himself and not the team. Perhaps most commonly: not English enough.

Every time Kevin Pietersen fails (where 'fails' can mean anything from a duck to getting out in the 90's going for a big shot to bring up his century), there is a pissing, moaning, wailing jeremiad from complainers demanding he be dropped from the England team. Finally, before last summer's limited overs series against Pakistan, they got their wish.

National selector Geoff Miller stated as the reason for his non-selection: "His form has not been where he would have wanted it to be, so we've given him the opportunity to get some middle practice – with the Ashes in mind...We need him to get his form back and we think he will do that playing some county cricket. There are a few players who will be fighting to get into that side, and Kevin will be one of those."

But whether some people may like it or not, it is really all about Kevin Pietersen, because when he is in form he is unarguably one of the world's best batsmen, and England's most valuable player. They will need him to display that form in Australia. Hence why no similar drastic measures for Cook or Collingwood, despite both being in similarly indifferent form (Cook scored a hard-fought ton during the third Test against Pakistan at the Oval but technically still looks on very shaky ground).

The reasons why many people dislike Pietersen irritate me. It is easy look at his flamboyant, aggressive style and accuse him of arrogance and selfishness; however, demanding he be dropped from the team seems a classic case of cutting off one's own nose to spite one's face.

These are the same Little Englanders who threw up their hands in horror when KP was made England captain. "But... but... he's not... English." When asked what exactly they think constitutes Englishness, no one can seem to agree. Born here? England's current captain wasn't born here. Neither was Douglas Jardine (born of Scottish parents in India), but no one seemed to give a shit about that when Harold Larwood was dismantling Bradman.

And as for length of residency, and whether or not you have ever pledged your loyalty to the team of your erstwhile country of residence, be it at junior or senior level, well, no one seems to be able to agree on that either.

Sometimes you think they just mean he doesn't have the right accent. If Pietersen is eligible to play for the England team, then he is eligible to captain it.

The issue of his captaincy is moot, now, of course, since the crisis that erupted when the relationship between him and coach Peter Moores broke down beyond salvation, leading to Moores losing his job and Pietersen his captaincy. The successful Strauss–Flower axis was a fortuitous alchemy forged in the crucible of that conflict, so while Pietersen contributed little to the 2009 Ashes series as a batsman due to an injured Achilles, it is arguable that England would not have regained the urn without him.

Dropping KP, and sending him to a second division Surrey side, seemed to me more punishment than opportunity. But it cannot be denied that his form is, at the moment, woeful – certainly by his own exalted standards – and once again everyone seems to have an opinion on it.

It has been seventeen months since Pietersen last scored a Test ton, against the Windies at Port of Spain in March last year, and although in 2010 he scored a 99 at Chittagong and 80 at Edgbaston, his Test average has now dropped below 50 to 47.80 – still extremely respectable, but a definite, worrying decline for someone with his talent.

The manner of his dismissals has come under scrutiny. He has been undone by left–arm spin, and, some would say, by his own hubris. His shot selection has been questionable and ill–timed, and distractions off the field such as the birth of a new son can hardly have helped to refocus his attention on it. They say Formula 1 drivers slow down after they become fathers, reminded perhaps of their own mortality and the awareness that there is a life beyond their chosen profession. England should be fervently hoping that parenthood has not slowed Pietersen down.

The fact that you are either wallowing happily in schadenfreude, or tearing your hair out with worry over Pietersen's recent slump, says everything about how important he is to England's Ashes prospects. If you are Australian, it also says everything about how much you fear him.

The Australians have already started targeting him in the

traditional pre-Ashes round of psychological warfare. Ricky Ponting has already named him "a big question mark", former Australia coach John Buchanan has said he could become "a major problem" for England, and has called him "the odd glitch" in the England team's consistency and mental strength. Even Mitchell Johnson has chipped in, promising KP a heavy dose of the short-pitched stuff.

Like I said, schadenfreude, accompanied by fear and respect.

The reasons Pietersen is disliked by some are precisely those qualities which make him so successful. By the nature in which he plays, he has never had a long, extended run of outstanding form. But the way he plays has also given us the flamingo shot, the switch-hit, the 158 at The Oval that helped secure the 2005 Ashes for England and more recently, the Man of the Series award at the 2010 T20 World Cup and an 116 scored in a Clydesdale Bank 40 game for Surrey against Sussex during his period of selectorial purdah. What makes him good, what earmarks him still as a possible future great, is a brash, combative style backed up with considerable talent-laden substance.

This current slump, this "odd glitch" is simply that: it is merely temporary.

Pietersen is still England's best batsman. The World Cup is upon us. It is time for him to make the world suffer.

And it is time for his critics to shut the fuck up.

LegSideFilth spews forth at www.legsidefilth.com.

Cricket Widows: How Cricket Has Ruined My Love Life

Whenever England lose, my husband takes it out on me.

What happened, darling?

"YOU FUCKING WHORE! WHAT THE FUCK DO YOU MEAN 'WHAT HAPPENED?'! RAVI BOPARA JUST SOLD HIS PARTNER DOWN THE RIVER, YOU FUCKING IMBECILE! WHY CAN'T THE WORLD JUST UNDERSTAND THAT HE'S A USELESS GOBSHITE?! WHAT'S FOR DINNER FOR FUCK'S SAKE?"

Whatever you'd like, darling...

"YOU TAKING THE FUCKING PISS? YOU HAVEN'T EVEN GOT DINNER READY? I HAVEN'T MOVED FROM THIS SOFA IN 8 HOURS, AND I'M COVERED IN TEARS AND THE STENCH OF MY OWN URINE: MAKE ME FUCKING DINNER, NOW!"

No problem, so what would you like me to make you?

"DINNER, YOU IDIOT, WHAT DON'T YOU BLOODY UNDERSTAND, WOMAN? D–I–N–N–E–R: DINNER.

MAN NEED TO EAT, WOMAN NEED TO COOK."

Any other woman would have walked out the door, but as a bona fide cricket widow, there's a part of me that is already emotionally numb. I just accept it, and am occasionally thankful for the rare make-up sex which may follow his inevitable grovelling apology – that is, of course, once I have summarily ignored him for the next six hours.

Occasionally, I find the poor bastard scrounging the fridge for leftovers, or ordering out. Shame the minimum delivery is £15 in most places, so he orders five extra garlic breads for himself out of sheer bloody-mindedness. Sometimes, he even tries to microwave leftovers, bless. Steve Waugh was right – mental disintegration does work on Poms.

All this is not particularly in keeping with my husband's character. By day, he verges on boring, which is not out of keeping for an IT technician. He is vaguely friendly but is essentially 'just there'. He was once disciplined for hacking into his boss' computer and planting a picture of Abi Titmuss as his screensaver, but the fall-out was so horrendous that he feels afraid to come out of his shell any more.

Apart from, when he comes home and turns on the cricket, which is precisely when he becomes a right arsehole.

27

His veins begin to pop out of his pasty white skin, his cheeks become cherry-stained, and he begins to howl at every misfield, no-ball, and of course, the tragic incompetence of Asad Rauf.

He demands silence, dismissively ushering me away should I come between him and his precious flatscreen – a TV which he boasts is 'HD Ready', but doesn't realise that we would have to pay extra for it to function as such.

When he is 'busy' watching cricket and I am thoughtful enough to bring him a fresh fruit salad or a cuppa, he will never engage in any form of eye contact. Nor will he ever use cutlery when eating food and watching cricket. The sport – I presume it has something to do with Kamran Akmal – truly brings out the neanderthal in him.

By this point in our relationship, it has become painfully clear that there is a depressing pecking order:

Cricket > Food > Wife > Beer

I also don't see why he is so obsessed with Shahid Afridi. We both have similarly luscious hair, although I do concede that I never get promotions at work for sucking at life and bending the laws. My partner is not even Pakistani himself, yet he watches YouTube videos of Afridi's Head & Shoulders adverts.

Confusingly, sometimes I find him posing in front of the bathroom mirror, stroking his ever-growing bald patch and pouting: "Because I'm worth it, *yaar.*" I daren't ask.

As if I don't have enough to battle as a woman who is systematically having her dreams crushed by society, government and partner, I am now struggling against this intangible yet wonderful beast of cricket. It has already sucked in my husband, and I am a slave by association.

My biggest regret at this stage is not moving to Australia after completing my law degree, which would probably have been a better bet than settling for a high-rise in Hackney, with what his very own workmates refer to as a 'briefcase wanker'.

My worst fear is that I will end up having to leave my dear husband.

My second worst fear is that during The Ashes, when the hours are inhumane for those of us outside Australia, I will be woken up by a banshee's cry of "HOW DID YOU DROP THAT, MONTY?!"

On the plus side, my twenty-something toyboy hates cricket.

The Cricket Widow drinks five glasses of red wine every day, and is suitably bitter.

Bridging the Divide

It all happened so quickly it was a blur. Yet, time seemed to move very slowly. The impact of those three deliveries left an indelible mark and the outcome wasn't in question any more. He wasn't going to let his team down. Not today. Not on this stage, the biggest of them all. He had spent countless sleepless nights dreaming up this scenario.

He just couldn't let his country down. It was only the second over in a chase of 274. At the end of that fateful over, there were still 247 more runs which needed chasing but the writing was on the wall. He wouldn't be denied in this quest. An uppercut for six, a flick to square leg for four, followed by a dead straight bat with no follow-through for another turf-searing boundary.

Game, Set and Match: Sachin Tendulkar.

It was past midnight, and the date was March 1, 2003. In the snow-covered grounds of central Pennsylvania, in the days when internet streams were as slow as an Inzamam single, three Indian graduate students decided to host a World Cup viewing in their basement rooms. They had installed a satellite dish and hooked up two TV's for people to come together in watching the only sport they dearly loved. It was 36th match of the tournament and so far, the general turnout for the games was only 8-10 people per match. They knew March 1st was going to be a different animal; it was India vs Pakistan.

Two hours before the start, there was only a trickle of bodies. A few here and there. But as game time approached, there were about 80 people packed in to two basement rooms. As it turned out, the population of the two rooms were divided along the team loyalty lines, and the folks cleared their pipes with '*Pakistan Zindabad*' and '*Bharat Mata ki Jai*' to open the match. Neither team could afford to lose this match. It doesn't matter if you don't win the cup, but just win *this* one. The nervous energy was palpable, both in the rooms and in the stadium. In a high pressure match such as this, teams want to win the toss and bat first. Advantage Pakistan.

We always hear of how sport is a great unifier, bringing together people fighting each other for generations for a match during which they still unabashedly root for their teams, standing side by side but at the end of the day, tip the hat to the winner and retire back to their quarters to resume their hostilities on the battlefield. It was one of those days in my household. A group of Pakistani students cheering everything that went right for their team and everything that went wrong for India, and the Indians responding in kind.

Even with the early reverses, Saeed Anwar who had no form to speak of coming in to the match, played in the only way he knows when playing against India – calm, composed and all set for a huge score. The Indian fans' joy at Inzamam's run-out was short lived as they realised the threat of Anwar. He kept at it unimpeded, and duly reached a well-deserved century. After he was out to a tired shot, mayhem soon followed, with Pakistan scoring 78 off the last 59 balls. When Wasim Akram was bowled by Zaheer Khan in the 49th over, the Indian side of the basement erupted, but when the camera panned to the umpire signalling a no-ball, the Pakistani fans erupted in incomprehensible joy with roars, which did not stop until well past the end of the Pakistan innings.

India had never chased a score more than 222 in a World Cup match before, and considering the pressure coming in to the match, the prospects looked bleak. The Pakistani fans had a swagger during the innings break and even offered to buy the Indians breakfast to ease the pain of a certain defeat.

And so they did: doughnuts and muffins were devoured, and hot coffee was gratefully gulped down. Both groups showed unwavering, passionate support for their nations, but never crossed any boundaries of civility and decency. It will remain one of my most treasured memories in a lifetime of watching the sport.

India's response began with a bang. Sehwag and Tendulkar were going hammer and tong at Akram, Akhtar and Younis, with India reaching 50 in 5 overs. The gob-smacked Pakistani fans once again found their voice when the wily Younis plucked out Sehwag and Ganguly off consecutive deliveries. A certain uneasiness pervaded throughout the rooms.

But when Abdul Razzaq dropped Tendulkar off Akram on 32 through an ill-timed jump, all the signs were beginning to point in one direction. As the innings progressed, the only question that remained in the match was whether Tendulkar was going to be able to reach a very well-deserved century. He batted like a dream, with high elbows, swift feet, supple wrists and all.

Eventually, a visibly cramped up Tendulkar was trying to hold on and continue the march. When Aamer Sohail bellowed: "If you can't get him out, at least get him hurt," both rooms in the basement booed. It was a sign of two passionate sets of fans realising that they were watching Tendulkar performing at the peak of his powers.

Sport played at its highest level, by players that reduce it to pure art form, can make two opposing sides forget their loyalties, and allow them to bask in its glow. Akhtar may have got his own revenge by dismissing Tendulkar with a rapid bouncer for 98, but the crowd of 80 stood as one to applaud one of the finest innings ever seen. India eventually got home with wickets and overs to spare, but the outcome was a mere footnote in the grand scheme of things.

Subash Jayaraman is an Engineer living in State College, Pennsylvania trying to fudge his engineering career to pay for a life of cricket – watching, pondering and writing. He can be read at The Cricket Couch and followed on twitter @cricketcouch.

Test Match Sofa or: How I Learned to Stop Worrying About Laxman Sivaramakrishnan and Love the Sound of My Own Voice.

*Test Match Sofa is an online radio station, offering Alternative live cricket commentary. Founder **Daniel Norcross** relives the birth of what has now become a daily staple for thousands of listeners across the globe...*

People often ask me why I started Test Match Sofa. They only ask once, however, because the answer is so long elephants go through a full period of gestation before I'm finished. So, when those truly splendid folks at The Alternative Cricket Almanack suggested I do a piece on the origins of The Sofa, I wondered if they knew what they were letting themselves in for.

My Project Manager role in a financial services company in London had fortuitously been made redundant in January 2009 (officially that is; I'd been pretty much a waste of money for the preceding two years owing to my own indolence and the company's legendary incompetence). As in all things related to the finance industry, my relative incompetence was rewarded with an undeserved payoff.

I had time to ponder my next move. Four months, I reckoned, would be enough to learn how to bake, get fit and plough through all of The Wire and The Sopranos on DVD box set.

I was pretty much right, except that I'd forgotten to work out what to do next. And worse still, I was enjoying leisurely lunches with other unemployed friends, my fabulous new cauliflower curry, the parallel universe of Baltimore, USA. The Ashes were fast approaching. My girlfriend was beginning to exhibit tell-tale signs of impatience tinged with jealousy and despair, and if I wasn't careful I'd be back drawing up fictional Gantt charts for pension-selling parasites before you could say "I think this upcoming series between two mediocre teams could be a real thriller".

Like all good things in life, Test Match Sofa presented itself to me when I was just the right side of intoxicated. It's like darts. I'm rubbish on no drinks and diabolical on eight pints but somewhere in between a flash bulb of inspiration switches on, the mind relaxes, and Archimedes' exultant cry goes up.

Sitting alone with only Pommie Mbangwa and Robin Jackman for company on the TV, I found myself repeating their inanities in an ever more furious fashion. "Graeme Smith will be hoping his batsmen can overhaul this relatively small total and deliver a win for South Africa." No. You're kidding me. "The crowd are really enjoying their day in the sunshine." Are they, really? How did you gather that? Did you ask them? They might be naturally happy people who are actually a bit more subdued than normal.

36

And what's it got to do with the sodding cricket? In fact, why don't you all just shut the fuck up and let me watch this in peace you banal, freeloading cheerleaders?

Everyone who loves cricket thinks that they could commentate better than the professionals. The difference between cricket and nearly every other sport is that they actually *can*. Listening to TV commentary had become an exercise in being choked by the bleeding obvious, whilst being brainwashed by broadcasters desperate for you to believe that everything you watch is of the highest calibre. Objectivity had been replaced with marketing. Wit and humour which used to garland my earliest recollections of commentary were now replaced by creepy old men making suggestive comments about bikini-clad fans in makeshift swimming pools. And the uncritical parroting of fan banners would have me reaching for my imaginary Uzi. It's not their fault. Playing cricket doesn't prepare you for being verbally dexterous and entertaining for seven hours, unless you're Glenn McGrath with a ball in your hand.

So I thought, why not do this commentary lark myself? Obviously I wasn't going to get a gig on Sky or Test Match Special. After all, I'd been cruelly overlooked for the England captaincy for my entire life. But I had played amateur cricket for 25 years and had a limitless supply of cricket tragic friends. Additionally, my work in the city had earned me contacts in web design and development. All I needed was some sound gear, a website and the cost of hosting a server. Oh, and about 20 willing volunteers.

You'd think that would be the hard bit, but surprisingly, the moment you say "I'm starting an alternative internet-based audio ball-by-ball commentary service covering all England matches and maybe a few high profile series from around the world, available to everyone in the world with an internet connection so nobody will have to worry about whether the rights have been bought up in their region ever again," pretty much all your cricket loving friends say: "Brilliant. Can I join in?"

So it came to pass that after a few weeks sourcing mixing desks and microphones from eBay, we were able to broadcast live for the first day of the first Ashes Test at Cardiff.

Initially we were a little rough around the edges, Manny excepted, who clearly emerged from his mother's womb complaining about the dampness underfoot, the poor light and the dreadful standard of catching on offer from the overweight midwife.

Perhaps we drank too much. Perhaps we were overcome by the excitement of the matches. And we had no idea how to structure the programme beyond commentating every ball and laying into Mitchell Johnson for having an overbearing mother.

By the end of the second Test at Lord's we'd hit our straps. The equipment worked. We even had a few listeners, who emailed in occasionally, saving us the trouble of making stuff up non-stop for eight hours a day. Insanely, we charged people £1 to listen, and cricket fans are nothing if not tight-fisted. Blowers may still have been mistaking Flintoff for Botham, but at least he was free.

Thus, come the South Africa vs England series, we decided to go free ourselves. We also held our noses and dived into the deep end of social networking by joining Twitter. I'm a bit of a Luddite and can't quite understand even now why anyone feels the need to inform the world that they're recovering from their cold, or could murder a cup of tea. But in terms of the programme, Twitter has been a godsend.

Suddenly, listeners from all over the world were sending in their thoughts, answering our statistical queries, setting the agenda. Unwittingly, they were doing our work for us. In addition, we hit upon the idea of recording jingles for players. This was the point at which the Sofa became addictive; for us commentators at least.

We'd always shown the players the minimum of respect. They are, after all, having a marvellous time and don't show it often enough. And much as cricket is a passion for all Sofa-ists, it is a game. So instead of greeting a new batsman with Laxman Sivaramakrishnan-esque hyperbole ("look at that marvellous strike rate of 81.2"), we decided it was time to poke a little fun.

Suddenly the true essence of Test Match Sofa was taking shape. We knew we'd offend some people but what would be the point of alternative commentary if it played by the same staid rules as the traditional broadcasters?

Listener figures began to grow. We hit a thousand by the end of the South Africa series. Then doubled that during the Bangladesh in March. Now we knew our listeners were crazier than us; 4am in March is no time to be listening to Junaid Siddique shouldering arms to a straight delivery. If you're getting up to listen to us yawning through the morning session, you must be committed – or perhaps should be.

We also splashed out on a syndicated audio player that could feature on bloggers' own sites so we didn't have to funnel listeners to our website. Suddenly we were on a roll. Jingles were being created for us by listeners in Munich and Mumbai. Commentators were emerging from all corners of the globe.

When at first, journalists and cricketers would ignore our calls, we were now getting guests with real pedigree. Iain O'Brien, the Kiwi quickie, came on for the ICC T20 World Cup and despite failing to pronounce Kapugedera right, showed us what an ex-international can do behind a microphone. His insights into technique and unguarded answers to direct questions were thrilling and refreshing. And all this was happening in my sitting room. Watching John Emburey dance to Umar Gul's sea shanty jingle will remain with me to my dying day as will The Wisden Cricketer editor John Stern's startling Alec Stewart impression.

And it isn't just cricketers and journalists who now join us on The Sofa. Comedians Mark Steel and Miles Jupp have been seduced by the fantasy of being able to commentate live. And that is the core of Test Match Sofa. Cricket lovers commentate their first game, usually in front of the mirror, as they imagine themselves scoring a hundred at Lord's, Eden Gardens or Melbourne. The language of cricket, the very means of describing it, transmitting it, lies within the soul of every lover of the game.

Test Match Sofa had started out as a means for my friends and I to indulge our own fantasies. Now I realise we've created something much better. A fantasy in which everyone, our listeners who tweet and email, the recently retired cricketer and the natural show-off comedian can all participate harmoniously.

So how long can we get away with living the dream? Well, we don't make any money yet, from our 18,000 listeners a day. And to turn Test Match Sofa into an institution we will need more sponsors and/or donors.

Test Match Sofa is not merely an alternative commentary in the same way as The Alternative Almanack is not just a collection of alternative views. They are both attitudes of mind; resistance movements at the vanguard of change. They will not stand alone. They will be joined by millions of the patronised and disenfranchised who all grow old in despair. Superior and inferior imitators will join them in storming the bastions of Channel 9, Neo and the rest. With a globally interconnected army they can and will challenge the lazy corporatism of broadcasters, the uninspired witterings of superannuated former cricketers and build a new Jerusalem returning cricket, that noblest of passions, to its rightful place at the head of all human endeavours.

As you will have gathered, Daniel Norcross is founder of and commentator on www.testmatchsofa.com, the alternative cricket commentary.

In Praise of...Tendulkar

As he walked off after sealing a convincing victory against Australia in the second Test at Bangalore, you got a glimpse of the other side of Sachin Tendulkar. Whenever I talk to someone from abroad about Sachin, the conversation invariably tends to focus on his batting exploits and the incredible pressure he must be under in trying to appease the expectations of over a billion fans.

In India, Sachin is loved for his cricketing exploits, but he is also loved just as much for his humility, in spite of his God-like status. As they neared the pavilion, members of the ground staff ran up to Sachin and Rahul Dravid to shake their hands and congratulate them. Rahul initially tried to ignore them and showed traces of irritation. In the commentary box, Sunil Gavaskar ranted about the ground belonging to the cricketers and said there was a place for fans to interact with their idols.

Neither Rahul nor Gavaskar were wrong and you can understand their mutual annoyance. But Sachin didn't think twice about it. As soon as the congratulations were offered and the trembling hands raised, he smiled and thanked the fan and shook his hand.

When India defeated England in Chennai after the terrorist attacks in Mumbai, a victory that meant a lot to him because it gave people something joyful to think about, he had reacted the same way when another groundsman approached him. Perhaps he realises how important these moments are to this fans and how little it costs him to shake their hands. Rahul had no option now but to follow suit. As is inevitable in these cases, two or three more people immediately tried to follow suit, and then a much larger crowd before security chased them away. But I have little doubt that Sachin would have patiently stood there and greeted them all, going by the stories I've heard of the man.

In April, an 87 year old woman, Saraswathi Vaidyanathan, who can be described as nothing other than a cricket fanatic, expressed her desire to meet him in her lifetime. Not only did Sachin go out of his way to meet her, but he even corrected her when she said she was lucky to meet him by saying: "No, I am lucky to meet you."

He apparently greeted her with "I read in the article that you have followed all my innings and know all my records. I need your good wishes." A month earlier he coached underprivileged children during the Joy of Giving Week.

You're probably tempted to say these are all just smart publicity stunts. But you'd be wrong. I've heard many, many similar stories from people who just by pure coincidence ran into him and summoned up the courage to talk to him. They always mention how polite he is and never declines requests for an autograph. He's been playing for over 21 years now, so take a moment to appreciate just how many such stories there are out there!

Millions of people treat Sachin's word as gospel and live their lives by it. A small tweet about supporting the fight against cancer raised a quarter of a million dollars in a day. When you are as successful as Sachin is, when you are as worshipped as him, you become an incredibly powerful person. It would be very easy to let your ego feed on that power and try and use it to your selfish advantage. It takes extraordinary magnanimity and benevolence to not just push your achievements to the background, but to also use your position to help everyone you meet and make them feel special.

He has remained true to himself right from the earliest days of his success when he was touted as a child prodigy but always responded by insisting that he was a student of the game and had much to learn. There will be tremendous pressure on him to become a politician in his later years as unscrupulous parties seek to profit off his popularity, but somehow I suspect he'd be happier playing backyard cricket with his childhood friends and their children as he still does in his spare time today.

Antony Chettupuzha/Achettup blogs about cricket at Short of a Length and for Bored Cricket Crazy Indians.

The Best Bloody Cricketer in the Whole Wide World

They say the art of leg spin is dead. Since Warney packed in Test cricket for Indian T20, TV adverts and some stop-off town in the Nevada desert, international cricket hasn't exactly been blessed with fine leg spinners.

To prove my point I could just mention Bryce McGain, but that would be harsh. Danish Kaneria is a genuine leggie but he just can't seem to cut it consistently at Test level. Amit Mishra was good, but not good enough for the Indian selectors. Steve Smith tries his best, bless him, but he has a long way to go. The fact is there is no Clarrie Grimmett, Abdul Qadir or even Mushtaq Ahmed out there.

Except for one.

Known to the casual cricket viewer as the guy South Africa tried to pick but then weren't allowed to, most would dismiss Imran Tahir as just another spinner. Indeed his profiles that circulate the internet happily back this notion up. 'A journeyman cricketer' and 'Never fulfilled his potential' adorn quite succinct, cold descriptions. It could be suggested that the people who have written these profiles have never seen Tahir bowl in the flesh, instead basing their presumptions on the number of clubs he has turned out for in his career.

And yes, he has been a bit of a tart in that respect. Charles Babbage constructed his programmable computer with the aim of one day calculating Tahir's number of clubs, as the abacus was not up to the task. There are more teams, spread out over Pakistan, England and South Africa that have printed shirts with 'Tahir' on the back than I can care to name, though the Water and Power Development Authority deserves a special mention.

Yet all of that is irrelevant in relation to his skill with ball in hand. For me, Tahir represents everything that I love about cricket. Here is a man who is not a gym freak like an increasing number of cricketers. I doubt he spends any more time than he has to when running and practising fielding drills. Batting is a bit of a laugh for him because his mind is focussed solely upon the talent that makes him oh so employable.

With one sleeve up and one sleeve down, a brisk canter to the crease is the prelude to a little bit of magic. Warne's greatest weapon was his stock delivery, though his variations were mightily effective too, whilst Kumble married the topspinner.

Tahir has full confidence in his leg break, but is equally adept at sending down the googly, topspinner among others. He also knows, down to a single delivery, when to bowl a particular variation. That is his greatest asset.

Often, when you watch a normal leg spinner (i.e. a crap one) you get the impression that a googly is bowled when the bowler feels like it, just to add a bit of variety to his spell. When Tahir bowls a googly, you are under no illusions that the previous dozen deliveries to that batsman have been bowled with the sole intention of making the googly the killer blow. There is no sledging, or staring down the opponent, or unnecessary outbursts of frustration. He is simply too nice for that.

That's not to say he is not passionate. Quite the opposite. All of those emotions, frustrations and feelings are stored up as the carefully constructed plan is executed, culminating in an inevitable victory for the man whose ally is his brain.
Be it the prize wicket in a final, or a tail-ender in a dead rubber, Tahir celebrates each and every wicket as though he had just found out that he has the only winning Euromillions ticket. Arms outstretched, head thrown back, shouting at the top of his voice and running to some distant part of the ground, Tahir is not only a joy to watch but he lifts the team around him.

I have always been sceptical of the idea of a talisman, as winning requires a team effort, but if such a person exists then it is Tahir.

In 2008, he joined Hampshire in Division One with seven games left. Hampshire sat bottom with one win all season and were almost certain to be relegated. In those last seven games, Tahir picked up 44 wickets at an average of 16.68, as Hampshire drew three and won four to finish third in the table.

He breathes life into a team, bringing exuberance, energy and everything one associates romantically with a sub-continental bowler – mystery, magic, guts and some cavalier slogging with the bat. I'd go so far as to say that he is the greatest leg spinner in the world currently. A lecturer of mine described watching a model steam engine in motion as "it's, well, it's orgasmic". He could quite easily have been describing the bounding grace of an Imran Tahir delivery.

Imran Tahir is a window to another time, an ideal that is very nearly dead. One that says "stuff your BMI readings," "to hell with your score on the bleep test". Who gives a damn about how many reps you can do in a minute? You're a bloody talented, thoughtful guy and you possess something that no number of coaches and back room computer analysts can teach.

The shape and size spectrum in cricket is sadly diminishing but there will still be those that champion talent over physical ability. Tahir is one and for as long as he plays, I will be in love with the diversity of cricket, and above all the art of leg spin.

Half-Tracker is a student who can't play cricket to save his life so he spends way too much time watching and writing poorly about cricket, Hampshire Cricket in particular.

My Irrational Hatred

Here is my brief list of modern cricketers who due to prejudice, envy, irrational anger, and despite, or even because of, many positive qualities, I consider to be deserving of the angry vitriol of an unknown cricket fan.

Shivnarine Chanderpaul

There are few more soul-destroying sights in cricket than watching Shivnarine Chanderpaul and Brendan Nash batting together to make a gritty century partnership in about six and a half days. This is not really Nash's fault. His God-given talent might be a great deal higher than most of us, but it wasn't enough to command a regular place in Australian state cricket, so it's understandable that thrown into a Test match, he prefers to place crease-occupation above aesthetics.

Chanderpaul, however, has no such excuse. He has scored the fourth-fastest hundred in the history of Test cricket, and has been known to play some sparkling innings at the top of the order in ODI's. He has the necessary talent to be entertaining – but alas, he wilfully chooses to be boring. He is renowned for enjoying batting, and it's almost as if he has chosen to eschew all risk, and all excitement, to ensure he bats as long as possible; a cover drive for four gives him no more pleasure than a leave, and sod the watching spectators who are forced to endure yet another dot ball.

His torture of paying spectators doesn't end with slow scoring however, as Chanderpaul has modified his technique to ensure that he's not just slow, but ugly too. Each ball he begins bent forward as if auditioning for the Hunchback of Notre Dame, lifting his bat up to his left in a motion only ever replicated by the clown on a miniature golf course, before scrabbling across the crease in front of his stumps in order to administer the inevitable block demanded by the juicy leg stump half-volley. There can be no more hideous sight in cricket.

And what's up with the stickers under his eyes?

AB de Villiers

I bet a lot on cricket, so many may suppose the reason I loathe AB de Villiers is his seemingly unending ability to cost me money. It would be bad enough if it was just his batting – he invariably scores runs when I've bet on his unders, or gets out immediately if I bet on him making runs. More than likely, he'll then compound my misery by executing a brilliant run-out or taking a magnificent catch just when I want the batting side to score runs, and prove that he probably is indeed the best fielder in the world.

It must be the money talking; after all how else could one fail to admire AB de Villiers? Dashing, batsman, brilliant fielder, wicket-keeper, forced to choose professional cricket over tennis and rugby, talented musician, good-looking...on second thought, surely only a twat could be that good at so many things?

He's also a committed Christian, and for those of us in Britain who feel deeply uncomfortable with religious belief – particularly religious belief which is practised any more openly than in the mind, or at the very worst a church – such evangelism surely suggests an attempt to cover up some sort of Faustian pact?

Proof of this stems from his amazing fortune with the decision review system against England in 2009. There were about six instances where he was out, but due to various wrinkles in the system, he remained at the crease. Sometimes he hit it, but the technology couldn't pick up that he hit it. Sometimes England had run out of reviews. Sometimes he hit it, but Daryl Harper was the third umpire and he duly got away with it.

Perhaps AB de Villiers is a lucky twat rather than a smarmy twat. But the fact remains: he's a twat nonetheless.

Eoin Morgan

At first glance, there's much to like about Eoin Morgan. He clearly has an ice-cold temperament, finishing countless ODI innings to perfection as the rest of the England team loses its head. Perhaps it's because he's not English, as he admirably demonstrated before the T20 World Cup Final when his lips stayed firmly sealed during the national anthems as Pietersen,

Kieswetter and Lumb all belted out God Save the Queen.

Unquestionably, he plays some shots of which he is the only one in the world capable of playing. He's great to watch, still improving, and seems to behave the right way on the field. So what makes him a so repulsive?
The real reason why Eoin Morgan is so loathed should be abundantly clear on www.eoinmorgan.co.uk.

I imagine that someone at Engage marketing services, the PR firm responsible for this most vacuous of celebrity websites, must have met Eoin Morgan to sign the contract, however that appears to be as much input into the project as Eoin has had. The rest appears to be the product of an afternoon reading a Wikipedia biography and a dummies' guide to marketing hyperbole, the best piece of which results in them using a ludicrously contrived (and now out-of-date) statistic to say that Morgan's ODI batting average for England after 20 games leaves luminaries such as Bevan, Hussey and above all Viv Richards, "trailing in his wake."

According to Engage, the only player not trailing in Eoin's wake is Ryan ten Doeschate. Perhaps they do his website too.

Shane Watson
Self-explanatory.

Muttiah Muralitharan

There is no-one less twattish in the world than Murali, with his boundless enthusiasm, limitless energy and ever-present smile. Right up to the time that he jogs up to the crease, eyeballs bulging, and throws down his doosra – especially if you don't pick it, and it spins past your Collingwood-esque nurdle to midwicket, clipping the top of off-stump.

However much it looks like Murali's arm straightens when he bowls his off-break, he's probably spent more time at the University of Western Australia than most of its undergraduates, and it has been shown beyond doubt that it doesn't straighten any more than any other spinner. As a result of these studies, the ICC set clear limits on how much an arm was allowed to straighten during delivery, setting one limit for spinners and one for seamers. So far, so reasonable – Murali isn't punished for the condition which prevents him straightening his elbow, but doesn't have an unfair advantage over anyone else either.

However, he then invents a doosra, spinning the ball the other way. After undergoing the same analysis on this delivery, it was found that his arm did straighten more than was allowed for a spinner. At this point, instead of telling Muralitharan that he throws the doosra and is not allowed to bowl it, the ICC decided to change its rules in order to accommodate a single player!

It is not, of course, Murali's fault that the ICC is so spineless, and had they asked him to work on the delivery and find a way to bowl it without straightening his arm he would no doubt have done it, even slightly unwillingly. However, by being such an obvious beneficiary of the ICC's never-ending ability to pander to the best players or the richest boards, Murali gets on the list. And in my desperate, angry way I can't help feeling Ranatunga had something to do with it – and he's most definitely a twat.

Suresh Raina

With international colleagues such as Yuvraj, Harbhajan and Sreesanth, Raina is perhaps a controversial choice. However, for deeply biased and unscientific reasons, I quite like Harbhajan, while Sreesanth is a spoiled child, and until Yuvraj can offer some sort of evidence that he actually wants to be a cricketer, he doesn't really qualify for a list of *cricketing* twats.

So Raina it is then, and I think the reason is that he seems to embody the new Team India – the swagger that has given them the confidence to get to number one in the world, but also the frailties, which make many people outside India doubt they're worthy of the ranking and believe that they won't keep it for long. The Indian side that has reached number one has played very little cricket outside of Asia, and while the bowling is considered the weakest link, there also have to be big question marks over the young batsmen like Raina on quick tracks. He is, undoubtedly, one of the finest flat-track bullies you will ever see. There is nobody better at plonking his front foot down the wicket and swinging the ball over cow corner, and there are few better at stepping back and lofting the ball over the extra cover boundary.

To date, Raina has played only a few innings for India away from the slow tracks of Asia, West Indies and Zimbabwe, and was memorably, magnificently shit in four innings in England in the T20 World Cup. Like India as a team, tours to South Africa and England will tell us a lot about Raina. Frankly, I'm not sure he's up to it.

Is this enough to make him a proxy-twat for the Indian team which hasn't yet proved it's as good as it thinks it is? Probably not, but he's pretty chubby too.

Stuart Millson: Living in London, but born and raised in Sussex which is where my heart remains particularly when Murray Goodwin creams yet another cut shot for four or Michael Yardy traps a hapless county batsman LBW with a non-spinning left armer. Having exhausted every other avenue of making a living from watching cricket I've resorted to gambling on it, which I'm still hoping will prove profitable.

The Greatest Ashes of Them All

Well, it's a cold old winter settling in, and with a tough Ashes series away from home, I decided to find a happy place and reflect back on the top five moments from the glorious summer of 2005. Here are our top five moments from the recapture of the urn...

1. Lord's. I'd been reading about Justin Langer's preparation. It was a monk-like existence of solitude, training like a demon. He stated that he's been sparring in a boxing ring, to get used to the idea of pain. The man even inspired Michael Clarke to ink a tattoo saying: "The pain of discipline is nothing compared to the pain of disappointment." A true Viking, Genghis Khan-esque sentiment. This, at the time from a superhuman Aussie team seemed like witchcraft – the all-conquering mysterious Aussies even trained in Yoda-like ways which we couldn't possibly understand.

Well, fast forward to ball two of the series. Steve Harmison runs in, bowls a vicious lifter that smashes into Langer's arm and instantly leaves a lump the size of an egg. For about two seconds Langer didn't react – "pain not relevant, pain not relevant" at which point he dropped his bat, pulled a face like a kid eating his first ever mouthful of Tangfastics, and mouthed something which couldn't possibly be repeated here.

Pain got relevant, and the spell was broken.

2. Edgbaston. Day four of an exceptionally tight Test match: the last over. Michael Clarke facing up to a visibly exhausted Steve Harmison. Australia are seven down, needing around 100 to win, and England are getting that sinking feeling. Australia don't lose wickets in the last over; that's for teams like England to do.

As the ball left Harmison's hand, even live, you could see something was different. First thought was that it had slipped and he was going to release a 93mph throat-high full toss; followed by a highly uncharitable second thought that it would be tricky for Clarke to command a fightback from a hospital bed. However, gravity got involved with the cunning middle finger slower ball and, as it seemed at the time, it crashed into the base of the stumps in super slo-mo. Even on my own, sat at home, there was whooping and hollering and celebration – almost premature, as it turned out, but with heroics on the last day, the series was ON.

3. Old Trafford. England, guided by a sublime innings from Vaughan, had a healthy first innings score of 444, and Australia were looking menacing in reply, with Katich and Martyn batting together, a long way behind, but looking steely-eyed and determined, with Gilchrist to come and lay waste to tired bowling given half a chance. A breakthrough was critical, and up stepped a man once compared to a wheelie-bin, to deliver his containment left-arm dronery. Wheeling away, Ashley Giles then suddenly managed to deliver a ball that Don Bradman couldn't have played with a dining table, which pitched just outside leg,

took a trajectory which defied all known laws of physics, and tickled the top of the off stump belonging to Damien Martyn.

In one moment, Martyn's world collapsed, and his face showed the sort of expression normally associated with eight year olds and quadratic equations. In the end, it didn't swing the match, but Giles' bowling, from an Australian perspective, turned from a tedious exercise in patience, to possible execution every ball for the rest of the series.

4. Trent Bridge. So many to choose from: Flintoff's clubbing century, Ponting's comedy outburst after being run out, or Simon Jones' five-for. Overall, however, there's only one contender. The Aussies are about 125 ahead, with Lee and debutant Shaun Tait batting, frantically scrambling to get any runs they can to challenge England in the fourth innings, with Warne licking his lips and the pressure of 20 years of pain on England. Lee's had a reasonable series with the bat, and looks well capable of adding another 30 to take the England target from "we should get that" to "I can't watch, please tell me when we've won". Australia are the ultimate team, with everyone willing to die for the cause, and all impeccably coached.

Then it all cracked. For some utterly unaccountable reason, Tait decides to walk across his stumps and try to flick Steve Harmison down to fine leg, and predictably, given his all-too-visible stumps, is cleaned up. Looking on the bright side, if it'd been an off-stump bouncer, Tait would probably have needed major dental work, but the simple indiscipline when the game could have been on the line suggested England had turned the tide.

5. The Oval. You know it, I know it, there's only one contender. It's not Pietersen, who gambled everything in a thrilling knock and won, or Flintoff, who bowled like a man possessed and held the line for just long enough. It's the moment Shane Warne spilled a chest-high sitter off Pietersen and, effectively, dropped the Ashes into England's lap. 20 years of resignation ran through the mind …. the mental picture of Warne's magic ball to Gatting, the hideous sight of the spin maestro dancing around with a stump in his hands after winning the series years ago and long, late nights listening to the radio to hear we'd been stuffed again.. Warne spilled it, and we had won the Ashes. To be absolutely fair, the Aussies were so dignified in defeat that it took a bit of the fun out of it, but then after a a reverse drubbing in 2006/2007, the flame was lit again. Winning at home is one thing, snatching the urn away is another altogether.

Paul Sculpher is a writer specialising in the world of gambling and casinos, who occasionally branches out into cricket. He still periodically turns out for the mighty Fair Oak CC of the Hampshire league, and is a perennial fixture on their glamorous annual tour of Port Talbot – by all accounts, as a cricketer, the older he gets, the better he was.

Why Can't Girls Throw?

I don't understand it. It can't simply be a physical strength thing. I know plenty of strong girls and indeed plenty of pissy weak blokes. Yet the vast majority of girls I come across simply can't throw.

I'm quite simply embarrassed when I'm watching women play cricket and we have to relay it into the stumps from the boundaries. There are plenty of theories that try to explain it. There is, of course, an element of lack of upper body strength and the considerable problem of breasts. But I'm not a weakling; I can serve a tennis ball at speed, I can leather the crap out of a golf or hockey ball and I wasn't blessed in the boob department and yet I can't throw a cricket ball anywhere near as far as the men I know.

The long and short of it is that girls simply don't throw from a young age and definitely don't do it over and over again like boys do. We grow up playing netball and hockey, or worse, doing athletics. Bloody athletics – running round and round a track for no reason whatsoever. One has to hope that with more and more girls taking up and playing the beautiful game that over time the throwing will improve. I really hope so.

There is no doubt that the women's game has come on leaps and bounds but I still hear the generally negative mumblings regarding its quality. Whilst having more and more girls clubs springing up can only be a good thing, I remain unconvinced of the artificial separation of the genders from such an early age.

Up and down the country men and women, girls and boys are playing mixed hockey and mixed doubles in tennis. We don't get worried about the girls in these instances. We don't worry they are going to get hurt or that they simply won't be up to it. I'm a hockey player, I regularly play mixed hockey and believe me, the boys certainly do not alter their game. They play it just as hard, they hit the ball just as hard, they tackle you just as hard as they would a man. Playing against boys raises your game. Cricket is no different.

I want to see the women's game develop and improve and undoubtedly the ECB have been much more enlightened than other international boards in having a centrally contracted squad. The fact remains that most of our current crop of female cricket stars grew up playing their cricket with boys; there simply weren't enough girls cricket around. I suspect the reason they are so good is because they played with boys not despite it.

It is patronising and short-sighted to think that girls can't handle it against boys. They aren't going to get hurt any more than the boys might. We need our batsmen to face the fastest bowlers. We need our bowlers to bowl against boys who have the power to dispatch them. It's how we learn, it's how we can improve.

We are encouraged at grassroots level to send our talented girls to girls' clubs rather than keep them with us in our boys' colts section. This is a fundamentally flawed ideology and will only curtail the women's game.

Lizzy Ammon is a long-time cricket obsessive who blogs at www.LegSideLizzy.com. During summer months she is either to be found at Lord's supporting her beloved Middlesex, or sticking dots in the scorebook at Barnes C.C.

The Men Behind The Ashes

In the same time it's taken Graeme Swann to become the finest spinner in the world, Australia has had more retirements than a Monaco GP. It used to be a case of turning on the telly on Boxing Day and watching players like Craig White literally lose the will to play international cricket. But how good are this current English team? Should the Aussies be scared? And do the Aussies have what it takes to regain the Ashes? *Timothy Bunting*, an Australian living in England and subject to all the English shenanigans, runs a fine-toothed comb over both squads and ends up getting it stuck in Dougie Bollinger's hair plugs.

England

Andrew Strauss

Conservative, predictable captain who has benefited enormously from Andy Flower's shrewd management, and seemingly has claimed the credit for himself. Immensely unlikeable, with an air of permanent smugness and not a shroud of charisma, he has a big ask to keep his reputation intact on this tour. Can't help himself outside off-stump and should provide catching practice for the cordon.

Fear factor: 5

Alistair Cook

We spent all summer listening to Nasser Hussain banging on about Cook's technique as he dangled his bat in front of his pad and edged the Bangladesh trundlers to the slips. However, he's not as bad as he's made out to be and is capable of the big scores, although doesn't have the disposition to frighten the Aussies. Would imagine he's a strong candidate for Australia's likely 'mental disintegration' tactics.

Fear factor: 3

James Anderson

If this series were held in England under greying skies with the Duke ball, the Aussies could conceivably be concerned by Jimmy Anderson. But it's held in Australia in the baking summer with a Kookaburra ball that doesn't swing, so Anderson is about as scary as a pot of basil.

Fear factor: 1

Ian Bell

Anyone who dyes their hair past the age of 25 is a prick. Add that Bell 'frosts his tips' and you end up with an unquantifiable level of prickishness . Typical Pom batsman who plunders runs in unimportant matches and then flounders against the Aussies. Has a rubbish record in Australia and the team psychiatrist should earn his keep from looking after Bell alone.

Fear factor: 0

Tim Bresnan

Big Bressy-lad should be loveable with his bustling action and unfashionable but effective batting, but he's like an annoying kid with no talent who keeps trying out for the football team each season and getting a place on the bench because the coach feels sorry for him. Then he spends all winter waiting for his chance and comes on in the last match of the year and scores an own-goal. Should be fodder for the Aussie batsmen on home pitches.

Fear factor: 0

Stuart Broad

Should be a hate figure with his stroppy, childish behaviour, but has characteristics that Aussies respect – aggression, determination and competitiveness. Doesn't help that he has a nice-looking girlfriend, something the Aussies could use to their advantage in their sledging, suggesting he 'punches above his weight' etc. Would be surprised if he hasn't lost some of his match fees by the end of the tour.

Fear factor: 7

Paul Collingwood

Like Bell, earns prick status for his hair dye, although doesn't look half as much of a prat. Has been in the doldrums for some time, continually falling away and getting trapped in front. Took a good catch against Australia some years ago, but is the wrong side of thirty and can't really see what he offers any more. Should enjoy the trip to Oz though, there are some really pretty sights.

Fear factor: 0

Steven Finn

Tall, strong and quick, Finn should be a real handful on Aussie pitches but has a horrible collapsing action and doesn't get the bounce his height warrants. Named ICC Emerging Player of the Year, but to be honest it was a weak field and the obvious candidate (Mohammad Amir) sort of blew his chance with some silly no-balls at Lord's. Has been hyped all summer long for taking wickets against Bangladesh, but that's like praising a plumber for correctly changing a washer.

Fear factor: 2

Steven Davies

A left-handed version of England's T20 World Cup winner Craig Kieswetter: in other words an over-rated, chancy prick. Tidier behind the stumps than Kieswetter, but flukey lofted drives that just land outside the inner circle are not going to worry the Aussie bowlers. Neither is scoring a bunch of runs in the County Championship, especially Division II. Unlikely to get a look in for the Tests.

Fear factor: 1

Eoin Morgan

Determined little leprechaun who has garnered a Michael Bevan-esque reputation for his ODI prowess. Like Bevan, has big question marks about him in the longer form and has so far flattered to deceive in Tests. Likes to feel bat on ball all the time, but it's not much good if it's off the edge and the ball is flying into the cordon. Expect catching practice for the Aussie slips.

Fear factor: 5

Monty Panesar

Loveable in the way one loves a three-legged dog, Monty should be a hit down under with his comical fielding and non-threatening left-armers. Supposed to be a bunny with the bat, but infuriated Australia in Cardiff last series. Still, if Monty is playing, chances are something is wrong with Swann, so the Aussies would be keen to see him on the pitch.

Fear factor: 2

Kevin Pietersen

Hasn't scored runs for years, and now that Warney has retired no one in Australia likes him. Has the double-whammy of being a Pom and a Saffer so should expect suitable vitriol from the fans. Fine cricketer, but has his head in the wrong place most of the time. One of the many current English players that can't help himself on Twitter, Pietersen made himself look a little daft when he publicly criticised the selectors for leaving him out of the Pakistan limited-overs squads. Aura fading faster than Ravi Bopara's potential.

Fear factor: 4

Graeme Swann

Has moved on from talented larrikin to arguably-the-worlds-best-spinner in a matter of years. Many tweakers have had their comeuppance in Australia, but this is his chance to truly be part of the elite. Famous for his Twitter banter with James Anderson, but you'd find funnier half-sentences in a pub on Brixton Hill.

Fear factor: 9 (loses a point for his non-threatening, comical underbite)

Matt Prior

One of the most underrated players in England, Prior has seen his limited-overs spot usurped by flashier and much worse cricketers. Very capable behind the stumps and has a batting record not dissimilar to the rest of the top seven. Hard not to like, but like Swann has an underbite that makes him look a little bit retarded.

Fear factor: 7

Chris Tremlett

Like Finn with a proper action, Tremlett was an obvious choice for the tour. Problem is, Australia has its fair share of tall, bouncy trundlers and I'm not sure any of the Aussies will be shaking in their boots at the sight of him. Interestingly, Shane Warne said in a recent article that if the penny drops, Tremlett could be a premier fast bowler. Problem is, that little penny had been dangling precariously for so long that it has now given up its dream of freefall and has gone for a coffee, never to return.

Fear factor: 2

Jonathan Trott

For such a fine stroke maker, Trott really is a dour prick. Spends more time digging a trench on middle-and-leg than actually striking the ball, his idiosyncrasies will drive players, fans and Ian Chappell wild. Already has a belligerent debut ton against the Aussies and is fit for battle after allegedly whacking Wahab Riaz with a pad at Lord's.

Fear factor: 8

Overall fear factor: 5

Whilst England have made large strides under Andy Flower, there is still some doubt over their ability to win in Australia. Sure, they deserve at least a little credit for recent successes and *swallows pride* 2009's Ashes victory, but it's as much a case of an unimpressive Australian team rather than a brilliant English one. England lack the threat of 2005 when they had Flintoff, an in-form KP, and proper quicks like Harmison, and we all know what happened then. Australia certainly needn't be scared, but they will have to be at their best to regain the fabled urn.

Australia

Ricky Ponting

In the mix with Shane Watson to be the most hated man in cricket, Ponting avoids the prize through sheer weight of runs. Question marks hang over his captaincy and now that many of the 'Invincibles' have retired, has been often shown up as a conservative and poor leader. Stubborn enough to want to lead Australia in the next Ashes in England, will do well to survive past this series. Hasn't smiled since 2005.

Does he have what it takes? 12,000 Test runs says 'yes', his captaincy says 'possibly not.'

Michael Clarke
The face of corporate, media-trained sports professionals, 'Pup' has grown up to be one of those loyal but annoying canines that constantly humps your leg in public. A fine stroke-maker tempered by the constraints of professionalism, his career seems a

71

bit of let–down after his bright entry into the Test arena. Possible captain in waiting, Clarke has spent the last few years sleeping with the right people (and one wrong person) to set himself up for the top job.

Does he have what it takes? Sort of.

Doug Bollinger

If 'Doug the Rug' had hair, he would almost certainly be dyeing it blonde and thus earning my hatred. But he doesn't, and his attempt to cover up his baldness with hair implants reeks of desperation and extra–marital affairs. I'm not even sure if he has a girlfriend, but if he does he should cherish her whilst he has an international career. A big, lumbering left–armer, he would earn a bit more respect if he would pitch the bloody ball up and make the batsman play, but that's a bit like asking a caveman to use his club for firewood in the middle of winter.

Does he have what it takes? Here's hoping.

Phillip Hughes

Christened 'the new Bradman' after his first couple of Tests, Hughes is an example of media hyperbole at its best. Recently spent time in the boxing ring with Anthony Mundine which isn't the brightest way to prepare for a cricket match. May get a look-in during the series and should expect to be fending off a load of short balls, most probably into the hands of the close–in fielders.

Does he have what it takes? No.

Shane Watson

Watson has grown from one of the most hated men in cricket into *the* most hated man in cricket. If it's not the incessant sledging, the over-the-top appeals, the flashy sunglasses or that-apparently- fabled-amongst-professional-cricketers dyed blonde hair, it's his general arrogance that is so unlikeable. Doesn't like it when the ball moves around, which makes him a strange choice as an opener, but has done well so far. Made it onto the honours board at Lord's for his bowling this summer, which is a little bit like giving Phil Tufnell an award for his fielding.

Does he have what it takes? Yes, but part of me wants him to fail.

Simon Katich

Watching Katich bat is like watching an accountant filling out a tax return – it's not pretty, but it gets the job done. Even dourer than his similarly gusty predecessor Justin Langer, Katich has been a veritable run-machine since returning to the side as opener. Hardly one to get the crowds streaming through the gate, nevertheless Katich is as important as anyone in the current Australian side.

Does he have what it takes? Yes, but that doesn't mean we have to watch him bat.

Brad Haddin

It must be tough to follow in the footsteps of recent great Australian wicket-keepers and Haddin is certainly making it look so. Has a respectable record at international level, but will always feel like the poor-man's (insert name of famous Australian wicket-keeper). Supposed to be the chirpiest of the current team, but even then seems like he's someone's younger brother with no friends desperately trying to fit in. Ironically, is at risk of losing his place to someone else's younger-still brother and needs to be in good nick to keep his place.

<u>Does he have what it takes?</u> Yes, but only just.

Nathan Hauritz

Watch out England! It's someone who has a bowling average of over forty in first-class cricket! If the shoe was on the other foot, we could expect a reputable newspaper like The Sun to come up with a headline like 'Horror-itz Show!' or 'Come in Spinner! (and get hit for six)'. Continually distrusted by Ricky Ponting (North, Clarke and Katich have taken more wickets in a Test innings), he's managed to keep his place in the team as there are no other viable spin options in the country. Which is strange, considering the legacy of Shane Warne (smoker, womaniser, drug cheat, etc.)

<u>Does he have what it takes?</u> To win the Ashes? Hauritz? You've got to be kidding me.

Mike Hussey

'Mr Cricket' is a nickname for someone who lives and breathes the game. Hussey undoubtedly does this, but he has become more 'Mr Backyard Cricket' after a prolonged run of poor form. Was also in the 'Next Bradman' category for a while and whilst one can imagine Hussey playing cricket well into his forties, it'll likely be for a low-level club side in which he'll piss everyone off with his endless enthusiasm and talk of the 'old days'. Needs some runs badly.

<u>Does he have what it takes?</u> Of course! He's Mr (backyard) Cricket!

Marcus North

Everybody's favourite comedy cricketer, it beggars belief that North has somehow kept his place in the side despite having no discernible international talent. Five years ago, 10,000 first class runs and an average over fifty didn't necessarily mean a Test cap from Australia, but now it seems they're giving them out willy-nilly. If he were English, he'd be a laughing stock in Australia. Oh, wait. He already is.

<u>Does he have what it takes?</u> Most certainly not.

Tim Paine

Has impressed with his maturity in his brief international career, but he feels like someone who was about to join a long queue, only to happen across a much shorter one and ended up at the front. Very tidy behind the stumps, he has a chance to play instead of Haddin, but may have to wait longer to get an extended run in the team.

Does he have what it takes? Possibly not just yet.

Stephen Smith

Another who has benefited from Cricket Australia's fast-tracking of players, if someone uttered the words 'precocious' and 'prick', I would instinctively think of Smith. He's neither a proper leg spinner nor batsman, and whilst he may well forge a successful career in the shorter forms of the game, if he plays more than a handful of Tests I will be genuinely astonished.

Does he have what it takes? I wouldn't have thought so.

Mitchell Johnson

Spent most of 2010 either getting a ludicrous tattoo on his arm, or suffering from the effects of getting a ludicrous tattoo on his arm. He's sort of like that cool older kid you wanted to be like when you just started school, only to realise he is a complete twat who no-one likes. Has one of the most inarticulate bowling actions to grace the Test arena. Needs to get his radar right early on, or whoever ends up behind the stumps will have to get some serious goalkeeping practice in before the series.

<u>Does he have what it takes?</u> Somewhere between 'yes' and, 'it depends if his mum is watching'.

Ben Hilfenhaus

Matthew Hoggard anyone? Well, Hilfenhaus is a little more dashing with the bat and definitely looks more like a lumberjack than Hoggard, but they are both cut from the same piece of wood. Has similar adjectives ascribed to him as Siddle, although one can add "excellent outswing bowler in the right conditions." Unfortunately Australia doesn't really have the right conditions, but he is blessed with a strong, consistent action and should land the ball in and around off-stump often enough to trouble the Poms.

<u>Does he have what it takes?</u> I hope so.

Peter Siddle

Is frequently described in the media with adjectives like 'big-hearted', 'strong-willed' and 'hard-working', which is another way of saying he's shit. One of the latest of the long line of Australian quicks who has likely picked up a lot of 'most improved' awards in their careers, Siddle is somewhere between Glenn McGrath and Merv Hughes but is neither accurate nor fiery enough to be of any use.

<u>Does he have what it takes?</u> Probably not.

Peter George

Tall and thin, George resembles more a foal than an international fast bowler. Has benefited from the selectors recent strategy of picking fast bowlers for international tours with no credentials whatsoever. Can reasonably expect to follow the Ashes tour around and may occasionally be on television in the background when the cameras are showing Ponting grimacing at another failure or Bollinger 'being wacky.'

<u>Does he have what it takes?</u> No.

Do Australia have what it takes? Maybe. Not terribly convincing, is it? I really don't know. Their batting is still world-class (bar Marcus North), and their quick bowling can be as good as anyone on their day. But their batting has collapsed several times in the last 18 months and they don't have a proper spinner. And England are all right. They have beaten Australia in all forms of the game in the last year, which must go some way to banishing whatever mental demons they used to have.

With so little between the teams, here's hoping that the decades since England won a series in Australia weighs heavily upon them, and that the Aussie crowds get behind their team. And it wouldn't hurt if they paid someone to knee-cap Swann before the first Test. Australia better win, they *have* to win, because I can't handle another winter of gloating Englishmen and smug tabloid headlines.

My overall verdict: I'm saying this through gritted teeth, but Australia to win 2-1 with the rain saving them in a Test or two.

Timothy Bunting is a cricket trader, tragic, and part-time medium pacer. Once attempted to commentate in the outfield whilst positioning himself under a swirler with predictable success. Maybe that's what happens in the IPL when the ball goes up in the air…

The WAG's Lounge

TONY GREIG: And it's drinks on Day Two of the fourth Test in this 3 Mobile Ashes series.

BILL LAWRY: YES, it's a gorgeous morning here at the SCG, with the crowds still flocking in during this first session. Let's now cross live to our new spycam in the WAG's lounge...

[Cut to WAG Hospitality lounge]

LARA BINGLE (Michael Clarke's ex-WAG): [Struts into room] Morning ladies!

RIANNA PONTING: What the bloody hell are *you* doing here?

LEE FURLONG (Shane Watson's WAG): Yeah, I thought you and Pup were dust?

LARA: Well, yes, we are. But me and *Woman's Day* aren't.

RIANNA: Right, well Pup's off to a slow start anyway, so you didn't miss much.

LARA: Typical. He's always been a slow starter. But he sure knows how to build an innings...if you
know what I mean.

LEE: No, I don't know what you mean. Sorry?

LARA: Oh, it was a metaphor. I was referring to ol' Pup in the sack?

LEE: Ah, I thought so. But I didn't think you were capable of making such a reference.

LARA: Trust me, I'm not. I just stole that line from him. He'd always pretend to be Mark Nicholas and commentate in bed.

RIANNA: Really? And did he refer to himself in third person?

LARA: YES! OMG, like always!

LEE: Well, it's not as bad as Shane. He's always so down on himself after a poor performance at home.

LARA: Like, hangs his head with his hands on his hips?

LEE: Yep, you got it. But he makes up for it when the team's had a good session. Just jumps up and down on the spot, screaming at nobody.

JOANNE NORTH: Well, at least your other half keeps you excited. I'm constantly planning to dump Marky boy, but just when I'm about to do it, he leaves me a bunch of roses on my bed, or something else which gets him out of trouble at the eleventh hour. I don't really know why I dated him in the first place, but now that I've committed to him, I 'spose I've gotta keep extending these lifelines. But what about you Tegan?

TEGAN BOLLINGER: Pfft. Since that bloody hair transplant, Doug's become all cocky in bed, so to speak. And it's even harder for me now – I'm getting used to a 'hair adjustment' of my own Dougy's rug didn't just come from nowhere, y'know.

The door swings open, as an attractive, but frazzled lady walks in and sets herself up near the food platters.

RIANNA: Hi, can we help you?

JODIE BLEWETT: Oh yes, I'm Jodie Blewett. Greg Blewett's estranged wife. Remember him?

RIANNA: Umm, yeah, I guess so. But why are you here?

JODIE: Oh, Greggy never really got over being axed, so he clings onto the game with his little Fox Sports gig. He wants to move on, but the Mushtaq nightmares just won't leave him.

LEE: Right. But it doesn't really explain why you're here.

JODIE: Just lifting my profile for my radio show…and the free booze.

LEE: Ahh that'd be right. Anyway, [turning to the lady behind her], who are you?

MRS MCDONALD: I'm Andrew McDonald's wife.

TEGAN: Who?

The conversation is immediately interrupted as the door flies open and a prim-looking lady bursts into the room, huffing and puffing, short of breath.

RIANNA: Erm, excuse me…who are you?

SARAH SWANN: [Huffing and puffing] I'm Sarah, Graeme Swann's wife. I just needed to escape the English WAGs room. He keeps making stupid faces at me from extra cover, trying to be funny [Puffing] Man, it gets so lame so quickly – I just needed to hide. Quick, get me a drink! [Ducks to hide behind the back row]

RIANNA: Really? You left to hide from your own hubby?

SARAH: [popping her head up from behind the seats] Well, him and Ian Bell's wife. I find cricket fucking boring at the best of times, but trust me, I'd rather watch Ian bat than talk to her.

LEE: Well, sounds like you need a drink. Go for your life, babe. Hey, does anyone know if Peter Siddle's other half is ever gonna show up?

JESSICA BRATICH [owner of Mitchell Johnson's testicles]: Ha. You actually believe she exists, Lee?

82

LEE: Hmm, no, I suppose not. That awful shark tooth necklace would definitely keep *me* at bay.
LARA: Oh, shit I've gotta duck off now. I just got a text – the Brisbane Lions are training next
door. Back in halfa.
JESSICA: Hey, let me come with you. Mitch's mum is staring me down from the stands.
LEE: And can you take Peter George's missus with you – she's spilling punch all over her school
uniform.
[Audio cuts back to the commentary box, with the camera panning across the girls as they leave the room.]
TONY GREIG: This WAG-cam technology is terrific stuff. Heaven knows what they'll be getting up to off-camera.
A silence falls over the commentary box.
TONY: Oh, for the love of China, somebody say something.
BILL LAWRY: You dig a hole, Tony, you fill it.

Of dual nationality, Adrian McGruther straddles the wonky fence between Australia and Trinidad & Tobago, yet lacks the trademark Australian ambition and is bewilderingly bereft of standard-issue West Indian cool. This cultural nomad has written for a variety of publications in Australia, Trinidad, Spain and Netherlands, including a review of Curtly Ambrose and Richie Richardson's reggae band 'Big Bad Dread and the Baldhead.' For obvious reasons, he didn't dare write a word of criticism.

From Zero to Hero and Back Again

Here is a brief insight into the depressing world of a village cricketer and how it can cruelly give you a taste of success, before you dragging back through reality and shit on your dreams...

At the tender age of just 24, I can safely say that my cricket life is all but over. Irreparable. Hopeless. Irretrievable. Like Ricky Ponting and his fragile Australian side, I can't see where to go from here.

But it wasn't always like this. It wasn't always this bad. You see, 2009 was where it all went right for me. And for a brief moment, I felt what it was like to be a *somebody* in the cricket world. A very small, insignificant part of the cricket world, it must be said. But still, at least I was somebody.

In a nutshell, I was awarded the 2009 Saturday First XI Batsman of the year. I was awarded the 2009 Saturday First XI Player of the Year. I was awarded the 2009 Sunday First XI Bowler of the Year.

I was on cloud nine. I was riding the crest of a wave. In my world, I was top of the tree – and not just some shitty apple tree, I mean a big fucking Californian Redwood with giant leaves and metre-thick branches. Sneering and grinning over the shit-munchers below me, with more smugness and contempt than

Simon Cowell, I could do no wrong.

Even when I scored my maiden Saturday First XI hundred and got so unbelievably bladdered that night that I made the no-brainer decision to piss up against the clubhouse bar, no one minded. Nobody even batted an eyelid. I was untouchable, and I felt like Freddie Flintoff during PedaloGate.

In my little world (leafy, quaint, pretty Surrey), I could do no wrong.

However, it all went wrong in 2010. Oh so terribly wrong, and it all started during early spring.

It was just a few weeks before the first league game. So what does everyone do before the season starts, especially if you think you're the dog's bollocks? Yep, that's right. You go out and buy all the fancy gear regardless of whether you need it or not. New helmet. New gloves. New spikes. New whites. New pads – those outrageous Adidas ones with yellow straps (I told you I was deluded).

I even bought a new bat. Not even a very good one that I particularly liked. Instead, I opted for the most expensive one. The more expensive bat will show everyone just how good I really am, right?

Even though I might be at the more deluded end of the spectrum, I know I'm not alone in this. There are plenty of forty-somethings who take a couple of wickets with their Sunday trundlers, and start to strut back to their mark in an entirely pompous, self-ingratiating ceremony. Perhaps they give the batsman a snarling stare, because of the cheek of the bastard to dare hit HRH for a boundary.

They walk up to the batsman slowly, and between frothing mouth and gritted, rotting teeth, whisper: "You're bloody dead, mate." The fact that he's only 14 is way beside the point.
Or what about when the same bloke is batting and has just hit a 50? He does what any other amateur cricketing prick does – he starts twirling the bat in his hand like a young Alec Stewart, and walks down the pitch before every delivery, prodding down bits of non-existent debris.

At this critical juncture, such a cricketer starts to believe his own hype. You start getting cocky, and a bit too expressive with the banter whilst sitting in the slips. If yet again, you're standing in the drizzle on the Saturday afternoon of the FA Cup Final and particularly pissed off at not being able to watch it live for the sixth year in a row, you might even pat a Colt on the head and say: "Don't worry son, you'll get there one day."

There's only one problem in this Field of Dreams. I wasn't the greatest of all time. I was just a poor man's Kevin Pietersen – but with double the ego and half the skill. It was all a fluke – a monumental, unfortunate fluke.

It's now 2010. You've batted 15 times. Your top score is 28. You've succumbed to seven ducks. A new captain joins, who is not only better than you, but on what he has seen, thinks you're toilet at batting and doesn't rate you as a bowler either.

You now bat at seven. You field at square leg. The prospect of you bowling at all is laughable.

The confidence, banter and arrogance which were once burning bright has been put out like an elephant pissing on single lit match.

You now have to hang on to your spot in the First XI with as much desperation as a Pakistani debutant. You're dropped. You're now sitting at the bottom of the tree; that big bloody tree with all the other shit-munchers, who now treat you with the same contempt with which you once treated them.

OK, so I admit it: I'm shit at cricket. By the same token, I can't live without it. And these are the reasons why people like me don't make it as professionals. Welcome to the world of the village cricketer. A 2011, Saturday Second XI cricketer.

Robert Hicks is a freelance sports writer with a dubious forward defensive technique. He has covered everything from county cricket to Premiership football, right the way through to the Tour de France.

A Day in the Life of the Pakistan Captain

"The players are mentally retarded, they don't know how to dress and they're not toilet trained." - Intikhab Alam, Pakistan Team Manager.

On tour, leading a depleted line-up ravaged by in-fighting and the spectre of match-fixing, Pakistan's captain takes us through a typical day at the office...

0800: Big match tomorrow, we play a President's XI. Big money riding on Shoaib Malik to poison the twelfth man with laxatives – he's really desperate for a game.

0815: Just sent the vice captain to give Kamran Akmal a wake-up call. Instead of knocking on his door, we chuck a canister of nerve gas through his window.

0845: Shoaib Malik keeps skulking around our hotel, placing shards of glass on our bedroom floor in the hope that he might get a call-up.

0900: Just seen the ghost of Bob Woolmer. Told me that if I shaved off Kamran Akmal's unibrow, the number '666' would be revealed, just like The Omen's Damien.

0930: Over breakfast, just told the coach that I can't go on as captain with so many disruptive influences. He reminded me that I had a duty to fulfil, and would stop giving me his inside horse tips if I resigned. I hastily retreated.

1000: Got 99 problems and Shahid bhai just ate our match ball. FML.

1030: Kamran just caught a ball without wicket-keeping gloves. He celebrated by throwing the ball a mile in the air. But he lost sight of it and it landed flush on his head. He's in A&E now.

1100: Slipped the hospital orderly a few notes. It's funny as hell to see Kamran high on laughing gas.

1200: Our daily 'ban meeting' with PCB chairman, coach and team manager. We decide to ban Kamran, Umar Gul, Salim Malik and Mohammed Hafeez, all for various indiscretions. We're banning Salim Malik as an example to other cricketers, and Hafeez because he whistled 'Don't Cha' by the Pussycat Dolls out of key. Umar Gul and Kamran were both banned for not being properly 'toilet-trained', according to our team manager.

1215: Ijaz Butt also wants us to sue Kevin Pietersen for saying how the spot-fixing scandal was a 'big shame'.

1251: Lunch. Our fitness coach is a porker himself so it's tough to take his advice seriously. Just the five parathas smothered in ghee for the batsman formerly known as Yousuf Youhana. He's on the 'Inzy Diet'.

1315: Afternoon training is supposed to start, but half the team have stayed in for a siesta. We end up playing a game of Kwik Cricket, which soon descends into farce as I see men in dark suits exchanging money on the boundary's edge.

1345: The game finished with Rana Naved bowling a massive no-ball with the scores tied. The men in dark suits nodded in approval.

1400: That was a tough training session, having to watch Fawad Alam trying to hit a six every ball.

1500: We're due a session at the gym, which starts with our lethargic players struggling to lift kiddie weights. Saeed Ajmal has some sort of hernia after attempting to lift the 2kg dumbbells.

1530: The dreaded Bleep Test ends within three minutes. Every time someone drops out, they rush outside, panting. As last one out, I went outside to see most of the team lighting up cigarettes and gambling on marbles.

1600: Net sessions with Shoaib Akhtar are very interesting. I love to watch his 50 metre run-up, and then pull out of my stance just as he's about to deliver. His crystal meth frog eyes are really bulging now.

1630: Ever since somebody explained the concept of a 'nightcap', the boys have taken it as an excuse to have a swig of whisky after every training session. People say that our batsmen play as if they're drunk, but in truth, they're just very tipsy.

1700: Selection meeting with the coach for tomorrow's game. Shoaib Malik bursts in and threatens to cut off his little finger if we don't select him for the match. This is the fourth time he has done this and
his hand is still intact. We've learned to treat him as if he isn't even there. He always leaves as soon as the coach asks me: "I'm sorry, can you hear something?"

1800: Just announced the team for tomorrow. All omitted players seem to breathe a huge sigh of relief; looks like nobody wants to play...except Shoaib Malik, who is now bleeding profusely from where his finger once was. As we exit the conference room, he occasionally receives a pitiful pat on the shoulder.

1900: After a hard day's work, we're relieved to gorge ourselves on another buffet dinner. Kamran Akmal is back from hospital. As usual, there isn't enough space at our table for him.

2000: It's the night before a warm-up game, so we're all out on the lash. Starting off with a few clubs around town.

2100: We have only two rules: no leaks to the media, and the Akmal brothers aren't allowed to speak when it looks like one of us is about to land some clunge.

2200: Shoaib Akhtar always has the girls around him. No mean achievement considering any girl would know that they're walking a tightrope of STD's. His favourite chat-up line is 'Does this look infected?'

2210: Akhtar pulls his first of the night, and he's promptly back to the hotel with the leggy blonde. The only screaming she'll be doing is when she takes a piss in the morning: "IT BURNS, IT BURNS!" I'm going to make sure we bowl first and give him a forced ten-over spell tomorrow.

2300: I never understand why the girls go for Akhtar over a humble, solid middle-order grinder like myself. Yes, I am engaged to be married, but everybody's allowed a little fun, right?

0000: Kicked out of a strip joint called 'The Glitter Club'. The Akmal brothers failed to heed the 'look, but don't touch rule'. You can take the boy out of the village...

0100: Most of us are smashed out of our heads on Bacardi Breezers and Cosmopolitans. Saeed Ajmal was paralytic after one Strawberry Daquiri.

0130: Uh oh, team manager sent me a text: "Why r u not back yet yaar?" I replied: "none of us can get to sleep. all taking turns to play brian lara cricket in akhtar's room. Cum in if ur not chicken ;)"

0900: Woke up with a pounding headache and stumbled down to breakfast, a good 15 minutes late. Expected a bollocking from the coach, only to see that we now have a total stranger with an evil-looking moustache in the 'head coach' jersey. He greets me without introducing himself, and I look quizzically at my teammates, who just shrug their shoulders and get back to eating. I ask: "Who are you, sir? What happened to Waqar?" The stranger replies: "Do you want to keep your job?" I nod along, confused. "Then know what's best for you: keep your mouth shut, young man...oh, and get me an all-butter croissant while you're at it."

Just another day at the office...

By Nishant Joshi

Cricket – A Love Affair

It wasn't love at first sight. I didn't plan to start giving a shit. I never meant to. It just happened.

Allow me to explain. I grew up in Sheffield. I'm not a proper Yorkshire lass, as I was consistently reminded; I was born in Chiswick in West London. Cricket in Yorkshire is special. It's hard to explain unless you've experienced it. Team sheets with 6 or 7 of the same surname on them: dad, uncle, sons, and nephews. Entire communities sitting on the boundary and of course, as a woman in Yorkshire, you either made the teas or you did the scoring. That was the deal.

My dad and my brother played for Sheffield Collegiate CC, a prestigious club in the Yorkshire League that produced a certain M P Vaughan plus a few other county cricketers. I was shit at making sandwiches so I ended up being taught to score at the age of 8. I didn't really enjoy it, but they paid me a fiver so I was happy to stick coloured dots in a book every Saturday.

Fast forward 25 years: lo and behold, I'm still sticking dots in a book every Saturday.

The years went on and by the time I was 13 I'd fallen head over heels in love. I don't think I can pinpoint the exact moment I realised this, but as I got to puberty and beyond, the girls around me wanted to date cricketers, whereas I simply wanted to date cricket.

I remained with Sheffield Collegiate until I moved back to London in 1999 where I immediately started scoring in the Middlesex Premier League and attending every Middlesex match I possibly could. Cricket in London isn't the same as up north; it's not better or worse, just different.

We grew older, but our love blossomed. Sure, we had our moments just as all couples do, but we ploughed on with more good times than bad.

It's proper love. The sort that makes you laugh and cry. It fills you with pride. It breaks your heart. It makes you feel sick. It's the last thing you think about before you go to sleep and the first thing you think about when you wake up. When you break it down, it's basically ridiculous. But then again, that is exactly what I think about conventional relationships.

Neither of us are consistently good nor beautiful, in fact there are days when we are just plain ugly, but just like in the fairytales, I hope that cricket and I live happily ever after.

By Lizzy Ammon

Australia's Next Top Captain

Ricky Ponting turned 36 in December. He probably has no more than three years left at the top level. The Test captaincy seems to be his as long as he wants it. But then what?

Michael 'Pup' Clarke, I hear you say. Let's assess his pros and cons:

Pros
*From New South Wales.
*A competent, though flashy batsman.
*The current vice captain of the Test team.
*About the right age (29).

Cons
*One of his cricket (and life) mentors is Shane Warne.
*Immature and unlikely to change before his reflexes and eyes go.
*One of his cricket (and life) mentors is Shane Warne.
*Prone to powder at crucial moments.
*One of his cricket (and life) mentors is Shane Warne.
*Off-field profile is too similar to Lleyton Hewitt.
*One of his cricket (and life) mentors is Shane Warne.
*He believes and behaves like he is destined to be captain.
*One of his cricket (and life) mentors is Shane Warne.
*Talks about himself in the third person.

Unfortunately, this is not the pedigree of a successful Test captain.

Allan Border, Mark Taylor and Steve Waugh were all statesmen of the game who commanded respect through their behaviour both on and off the field. While Ricky Ponting can sometimes divide opinion, he too may assume cricket royalty status before his time is up.

Sadly, Michael 'Pup' Clarke doesn't have the same gravitas. Sure he now averages around 50 with the bat, sure he has Cricket Australia's marketing department purring like a kitten and sure he can use his feet to the tweakers. But he's Michael Clarke.

You may recall that this is the same Michael Clarke who:

1. Wanted to expedite post-Test match celebrations at the SCG in 2009 so he could dash off to accompany his fiancée (at the time), presumably to some A-List (or Z-list) event.
2. Tattooed the initials of his fiancée (at the time) on his shoulder and so sheepishly showed the world.
3. Said: "I like tattoos. My theory is that if I'm going to get one it has to be meaningful." So it has to be meaningful eh? Well that's reassuring. And he has a theory too. Why Pup, you're so clever.
4. Has his own management team. Do you think Simon Katich has a management team?

Still not convinced that Pup ain't the right man for the job? Well, at the presentation of the Allan Border Medal in 2009, only one of the four people on the stage was clearly out of his depth and looked only too pleased to be there. And it wasn't that talentless uber-smooth jibberer from Channel Nine, Mark Nicholas.

So who do we turn to as Australian Test captain?

Bowlers and keepers have enough on their plate so we can rule them out. Of the current set up, the two obvious candidates are Michael Hussey and Simon Katich. With both of them less than a year younger than the incumbent, they're probably not realistic options.

Shane Watson? He would be eliminated based on the likelihood he will almost certainly dislocate a shoulder pushing aside the shower curtain or bump his head on the wind chimes in the lead up to a series-deciding Test.

That leaves us with the likely prospect that the next Test captain is currently an outstanding Shield batsman who is no older than about 28 now. If he has captaincy experience under his belt by the time Ponting retires, then his stocks will rise further.

A non-exhaustive list of players that may fill the void include Cameron White, Shaun Marsh, Michael Klinger, Callum Ferguson and Phillip Hughes. I sense a furrowed brow or two.

After all they only have eleven Test caps between them and three of them have yet to play a Test. Who knows how many more caps they will have won by the time the next skipper is required.

So what's the form guide say on these contenders?

Cameron White – well regarded tactician (current VC under Pup in one day squad), impressive captaincy record at Shield level. Bats at four for his state and has well disguised leg-spin bowling in his kitbag. Played four tests v India in India in 2008 as a "bowling" allrounder. Five wickets at 68 apiece (including Tendulkar twice!), suggests bowling needs work. Also explains no more tests since. Averaged 29 with the bat, coming in at eight in those four Tests. First class batting average is 42 and 40 with the ball. Summary: at 27, age is on his side. Not among the top six batsmen in the country. Would be the England captain already based on his record, but hard to see him as next Test skipper for Australia. Being Victorian with blond hair may be the final nail.

Shaun Marsh – no Tests. Reasonable performer in his 30 odd ODIs as opener, but that's hardly a formguide. 20/20 record is better still, placing him further away from the Test squad and its captaincy. First class average of 36 not good enough. Summary: Needs to come good soon if he is to press his claims. Same age as Cameron White, but well behind him in the pecking order.

Michael Klinger – no Tests. Aged 30 and is now captain of his adopted state, South Australia, in Shield cricket. Has averaged 67 with the bat after the switch in 2008. Class or form? Averaged 26 before he switched. Suggests form. Summary: Well credentialed as state skipper, in form and about the right age. Provided he can transfer first class performances to Test level (more or less), Klinger could be the straddle skipper until a real one is discovered. Also unlimited opportunities for M*A*S*H puns for sub-editors across the country. Key factor.

Callum Ferguson – no Tests. South Australian by birth. Summary: Hmmm…South Australian skipper? Not tonight Josephine.

Phillip Hughes – 7 Tests, averaging over 50. Hails from **NSW** – big bonus. Diminutive, aggressive, left-handed and enigmatic. Looks ungainly and streaky, but a century in each innings in his second Test at Durban was head-turning. Has continued to look ungainly and streaky since and has only passed 50 once in his next (and last) nine Test innings. Less head-turning. Enigmatic. First class average over 55 suggests there may be something there. Technique floundered under sustained bumper barrage in last Ashes series. Enigmatic. Summary: Has an eye like a fish but can sometimes bat like a fish out of water. If he learns to deal with the short stuff, at 22 years old, this genuine pup may be the long term solution. Either that or he'll never play another Test. Who knows?

So, while it is not obvious now, in all likelihood somebody will emerge from the pack and move seamlessly into the role. What is more obvious, however, is that Michael "Pup" Clarke should stay firmly in the pack.

Who's it going to be?

Aram Margarian is a former stockbroker whose sporting ambitions were only limited by his on-field ability. His dream of batting in the middle order for Australia lasted until he realised that there were at least ten better cricketers in his year at high school. Not to mention the little matter of the Waugh brothers. His dream of playing centre-half for the Italian national team were thwarted when he realised that the lack of any family links to Italy may prove insurmountable. These days, when he's not three-putting from two feet at his home golf course, he manages to fit in amateur sportswriting into his almost hectic schedule. He does not have a life coach.

The Commentator's Curse

While the rest of the game progresses, the decline of cricket commentary in recent years has been tragic. Endemic of all that is wrong with our beloved sport, commentators have by and large been morphed into corporate slaves. They are zombies, but not the harmless nine-to-five office drones; these guys are Dawn of the Dead motherfuckers who will lurch towards you ominously and back you into a corner, before feasting on your own flesh in front of your own eyes.

If they catch you, you should be thankful if they eat you alive. For if they don't, you will surely become infected, and spread the scourge of cricketing *ennui* across the world.

For those of us foolhardy enough to skip a day of work or school in order to brave an Abu Dhabi ODI, I simply feel that we deserve a bit more respect.

There are various classes of commentator who have managed to, for the most part, piss us off:

The Channel Nine Commentators

The only thing we hate more than Australian cricketers is when they retire and actually start to open their mouths on air. Not only do they highlight their absolute ineptitude and lack of knowledge about the game, but they perfectly highlight why the rest of the cricketing world mutter 'twat' under their breaths whenever an Aussie cricketer walks past.

There are so many twats in Australian cricket that they may be distinguished into sub-species of twat:

Humble Sheffield Shield journeyman < Played one Test for Aus < Aus opening batsman < Ricky Ponting < Brad Haddin < Aus Commentator < Steve Smith < Shane Watson

Ian Healy, Ian Chappell, Shane Warne...all twats of the highest order. Somehow, in what is an Australian Old Boys club, Channel Nine have managed to also rope in Mark Nicholas, who takes the art of being a twat to new levels. The poor Aussie commentators would have to wait for Ricky Ponting's retirement in order to witness such excruciating 'Has he stopped talking yet?' commentary.

Expect to hear unrivalled insight such as "if the sun came out it would be a perfect day for cricket," and "gee whiz, they'll be wanting some early wickets here".

Richie Benaud is the sole shining light in the Channel Nine set-up. Never failing to voice his opinion, Richie offers a rare, non-grating antipodean accent. However, when you have one of the great players and commentators of the game being renamed as

'Betfair Richie' for the purposes of a broadcast, you know when cricket has sold its soul.

Sky Commentators

The pick of the bunch, The Sky Commentators are generally a joy to listen to. Ably anchored by David Gower, Sky have assembled a team full of former England captains, as well as David Lloyd and Michael Holding. They wisely use guest commentators to give us variation as well as balance.

Hussain and Atherton have both become brilliant analysts, offering us unbiased honesty and unparalleled insight. The banter between them is full of dry wit, with Hussain often being the butt of jokes for his perceived stinginess.

David 'Bumble' Lloyd has become an all-time legend in the field, always insightful and the undisputed king of banter. He has the perfect blend of analysis, honesty and humour, and it's hard not to admire this loveable old rogue.

However, Michael Holding is the reason that housewives tune into the show – his Jamaican molasses drawl is one of the few West Indian accents that we can readily understand without wondering what herb he's been smoking. He has no loyalties to anybody, and as such he is openly critical in ways which other commentators often shy away from. He never beats around the bush, and where 'Whispering Death' once struck fear into the hearts of batsmen, he could now be a cricketing hero for his commentary alone.

He would also make a better narrator than Morgan Freeman. Imagine 'Flight of the Penguins' with Holding waxing lyrical. Imagine "Deh penguins ah jummpin' into dah sea, yah mon!"

However, the major weak point in Sky's team is undeniably Sir Ian Botham. For one of the greatest all-rounders in history, along with his wealth of experience and gravitas, he is an exceptionally poor commentator. He stumbles over his words, lacks enthusiasm, and we get the uncomfortable feeling that he's talking down to us from his lofty perch. Botham's pitch reports are a regular source of embarrassment, as it is painfully apparent that he has no clue what he's talking about – come Day 5 of a Test match, he just takes a 20 pence piece and puts it in one of the crevices, before proudly announcing: "Did you see that? Can you see that? That's *incredible!*" Botham will then stare intently at the small crack in the pitch for a good minute or so, failing to realise its irrelevance as it is about four feet wide of the stumps. He is proof that a great player does not make a great commentator, and he is regularly embarrassed by Hussain and Atherton.

Also, one cannot ignore the sheer vileness of Nick Verity Knight, who seems to cover every single county game throughout the entire season. He is the type of man who believes every woman fancies him, when in fact no woman fancies him. Sky wonder why their county viewing figures are so low, but the answer is simple: Verity is an odious dickhead, and we all put him on mute any time he threatens to violate our ears. He is the very definition of 'banal', and if there were awards for stating the obvious, Verity would have been a lifetime achievement contender years ago. Yes, we know you know that you 'need to attack in the first 15 overs', and yes, we know that 'you can't take too many risks against a quality bowler like [insert Warwickshire player of dubious quality].' Moreover, we know that in a commentary world full of pretentious arseholes who all think they're the best at what they do, Verity is universally despised.

Then we have the second tier of Sky commentators, who are always confined into a studio, never to see the light of day. Led by Charles Colville – who is still bitter about not having been England captain – he is often joined by the likes of Rob Key, Ian Harvey and Jeremy Coney. Colville often comes across as arrogant but the poor guy doesn't know better. Having been brought up in a public boarding school, he is somewhat of a posh stereotype, but there's no denying that this man knows his cricket.

Key and Harvey are adequate placeholders, but Coney's knowledge and analysis is the best in the game. It's a minor tragedy that he's not given more airtime.

The Sell-Outs

Watching the 43rd ODI of the year between Sri Lanka and India? Well, you're most likely listening to Danny Morrison explaining how Sri Lanka's 18th choice medium pacer is showing great promise.

The height of banality, The Sell-Outs use clichés in order to bore us into submission, before assaulting us at our weakest point with a barrage of unsubtle hints to buy a Honda motorcycle, buy everything Sony, and do something abstract like fornicate or open car dealerships with Citibank and Airtel.

Laxman Sivaramakrishnan is like a creature from Middle Earth on microphone, but with Ramiz Raja, Pommie Mbangwa, Tony Greig and Sanjay Manjrekar, they're like a hoard of goblins beneath the bridge, snarling and sneering over the airwaves.

Aamer Sohail just can't speak English remotely well enough to be commentating for a living. Thick accents are fine, but not being able to pronounce 'Lonwabo Tsotsobe' and only referring to him as 'the new guy' is surely not on. The lack of tactical awareness is nothing short of astonishing, to the extent that we wonder whether we are watching the same game.

I watched all 51 games in the first edition of the Indian Premier League as a self-experiment, in order to see how quickly I would become fed up of watching top-edges going for six. I had a relatively high tolerance level, but around Day 24, I began to experience bouts of nausea whenever Pommie Mbangwa tried to make small talk with a shy Indian player on the sidelines.

"So, Rajasthan Royals are 180/0 after 15, and Chennai Super Kings need 10 more runs with 5 overs left – do you think that your boys still have a chance of bowling them out?"

"Erm...I think...this is cricket yaar...we will always have a chance, yaar...anything can happen...this is cricket, yaar?"

"You had a good match with the bat, scoring quick runs at the death, you must be pleased?"

"Erm, I'm the physio, but yaar, yaar."

Like nails on a chalkboard, it really is car-crash stuff.

We also have to wonder whether these has-beens are clinically blind. Few things are more infuriating than a batsman hitting the ball in the air, and listening to Tony Greig:

"OH MY WORD HE'S HIT THAT A LONG WAY; THAT'S HUUUUGE! THE FIELDER IS WATCHING IT SAIL OVER HIS HEAD!...IT'S COMING STRAIGHT FOR US IN THE BOOTH: WATCH OUT POMMIE! IT'S A

MONSTER! Oh and it's caught, 20 metres in from the boundary...what a shame for the batsman."

Ravi Shastri is their slave driver. The Darth Vader of a crew of worthless peons. Shastri used to be known for being a suave, sophisticated player whom the ladies used to swoon for. He also used to be a bloody good, unbiased commentator, with a towering knowledge of the game. The sheer weight of his authority in the game commanded your respect. At 6'4", he is the fourth tallest living Indian.

Even his voice was beautiful – as sexy as an Indian man's voice could possibly be. We even forgive his moustache, which veers teasingly between 'Bollywood villain' and 'German 60's sitcom actor'. However, being the agent for so many Indian players, he has a huge conflict of interest. It has been a slippery slope for Shastri, and during the IPL it seemed as if his very soul had been possessed by the devil himself, or Lalit Modi.

Ravi, if we ever require a voice-over for a porno, we know who to call.

In summary, in order to become a commentator in the 'has-been' category, you need to fulfil some criteria.

You must have:

- A frustrating career with unfulfilled talent, and/or plenty of chips on your shoulder.
- A willingness to deny Tiananmen Square ever happened (once the Chinese Premier League takes hold).
- Speech and/or visual impairments.
- Such poor grammar that no school would even hire you as their cricket professional/P.E teacher.

You must, of course, pass the stringent interview. This involves a mock airplane flight: the plane is spiralling towards the sea, and all life jackets are in your possession. Minimum sales should be seven life insurance contracts and eleven new bank accounts per life jacket, before the plane hits the water.

By Nishant Joshi

The Pace vs. Spin Myth

Myths become myths because they are peddled by believers. The Loch Ness Monster, WMD's in Iraq, and so on. And there is no bigger fallacy in cricket than the belief that pace bowlers are the most effective T20 bowlers.

Despite T20 being over half a decade old, captains, coaches and commentators still haven't quite figured this out. Time and time again, we see medium-pace trundlers getting smashed all over the park, dishing up length balls to brutes like Kieron Pollard and watching the leather disappear out of the stadium. We see Tim Bresnan huffing and puffing at one end, while at the other, the dour non-spinner Michael Yardy is going for barely a run-a-ball.

We watch teams get down to The Death Overs and throw the ball to Albie Morkel only to be flummoxed when he concedes sixteen runs.

It is a myth constantly peddled by commentators and fans. When a spinner bowls in the PowerPlay, the commentators describe it as 'risky.' When one bowls at The Death, it's called a 'brave captaincy decision.' During the T20 Champions League, viewers were asked in a poll if Chennai were too reliant on their spinners? Over 80% said yes. Yet Chennai were IPL and CLT20 Champions in 2010, often with three frontline spinners in their attack.

The myth simply isn't true. Top wicket-taker in the IPL? Praghan Ojha. The Champions League T20? R Ashwin. In other major events in 2010, spinners were amongst the top wicket-takers in the T20 World Cup (Smith, Ajmal and Swann in the top five behind Nannes and Langeveldt) and the Friends Provident T20 (Briggs and Parry second and fourth behind Thomas and of all people, Pollard). The only T20 tournament in 2010 that didn't feature spinners taking loads of wickets was the Standard Bank T20 in South Africa where poor old Nicky Boje languished in seventh place. But if Paul Harris is the number one spinner in the country, one can see how this happened. And it's not all about wickets. Top economy rates in the CLT20? Herath, Murali, Botha. IPL? Ashwin, Vaas, Kumble. T20 World Cup? Tait, Vettori, Harbhajan [minimum qualification 15 overs].

One of the reasons spinners are more effective is simply pace, or lack of it, on the ball. When fast scoring is required, most international cricketers prefer the ball coming onto the bat. It opens up run scoring areas down to third man and fine leg, meaning that batsmen don't need to generate their own pace.

One doesn't even need to be able to spin the ball. Some of the most useful T20 bowlers are simply slow bowlers who vary their pace and line and length. Michael Yardy, Johan Botha and Ajantha Mendis hardly turn it at all, but are some of the best T20 bowlers around.

Thankfully, some forward-thinking cricketers are trying to subvert the myth. MS Dhoni, not always one that seems an entirely convincing leader, nevertheless has been relatively bold and progressive with his management of spinners. Of course, Chennai are coached by the astute Stephen Fleming, who I'm sure has a strong influence on Dhoni's decisions, but its nevertheless been refreshing to see a movement away from traditional thinking.

Chennai played three frontline spinners for key matches of the IPL and weren't afraid of using them at the beginning and end of the innings. Zimbabwe have realised that their troupe of honest medium-pacers were fodder and built a predominately slow-bowling attack led by the aggro left-armer Ray Price and managed some good victories in 2010. Pakistan entrusted Saeed Ajmal to bowl at the death and very nearly made it to the final of the World Cup.

But, it wasn't all plain sailing for our spin advocates. MS Dhoni was lambasted for bowling Ashwin in the Super Over of a CLT20 match against Victoria, which David Hussey hit for a million. Shahid Afridi was criticised after the other Hussey pulled off a remarkable last-over victory against Ajmal in the semi-final of the T20 World Cup. These rare, but headline-making events undid a lot of good work. Suddenly everyone forgets how good the spinners have been and revert to their tired strategies; "Let's bowl Vinay Kumar at the death," "Give Pollard some length balls",

"Need a wicket? Throw the ball to Mitchell Johnson."

Of course there's a place for quality fast bowlers in T20. Umar Gul, Dirk Nannes and Lasinth Malinga are as effective as any top spinner. But as Zimbabwe have figured out, an average spinner will generally be more effective than an average pace bowler. Make the batsman earn their runs. There are few better sights in cricket than a batsman coming down the wicket and lofting a spinner for a straight six.

Or the same batsman trying a repeat next ball and being stumped.

By Timothy Bunting

Guide to Being a Proper County Tragic

English Domestic cricket is a glorious thing. Here's my guide to being a proper county cricket tragic (CT). Something we all aspire to.

1) **Membership of your county**

Paying to be a member of your county is obligatory. To be a proper CT you would rather sacrifice feeding your children than your annual membership subscription.

2) **Attire**

At the beginning of each season you must rush to the club shop and purchase one of each of the following

- Replica shirt for each of the three formats. Make sure these don't quite fit you properly. You must wear one of these shirts to all matches and events and probably to work and socially too.
- A cap – probably the T20 one as this likely to be the most garish one. Make sure you wear this not just to matches but to every social event, even ones to which you are wearing a suit.
- To matches you must make sure that you wear your replica shirt with something on the bottom half that doesn't in

anyway match the shirt – usually CT's like to wear brightly coloured patterned shorts.

- To take your tragedy to the next level you must make sure that you don't wash your hair for 3 days before a game and wear sandals with white socks or if you must show your toes, make sure your toe nails need cutting.

3) Autograph hunting

It is essential you spend your matchdays loitering around where the players are practicing or sitting during the match. Make sure you pester them to sign your almanacks, scorecards, programmes, autobiographies, 4/6s cards and whatever you can lay your hands on. It's always best to make sure you pester them at the most inappropriate moment, like when they've just got out. They love that.

4) Social media

In order to be a proper CT , you must make sure you facebook friend request every player and coach from your own county club. If they don't accept your friend request, it is perfectly legitimate to keep requesting and to shout something at them whilst they are fielding on the boundary. If they do happen to accept your friend request, you are almost compelled to comment on every status update they make and to tag them in lots of photos.

117

Similarly, make sure you follow every professional cricketer that is on twitter and reply to their every tweet no matter how banal. Don't be disheartened if they don't reply to you and don't follow you back. Keep persisting. Cricketers like nothing more than being stalked by the CTs.

5) Planning your season

If you have a job (and many CT's count working as an unnecessary evil that gets in the way of cricket), you must sit with your holiday booking form in your hand when the fixtures are released in January and use up all of your holiday entitlement to go and watch your county – all formats, all venues. Of course, your holiday entitlement will not be enough days to cover all the days of cricket so it is perfectly legitimate to ring in sick for the other days.

The true CT looks at second team and Under 19 fixture lists too and when the 1st team aren't playing will ensure they take their deckchair and picnic to those matches.

6) Statistics

It almost goes without saying that you must at all times be able to recite statistics from any point in your county's history. You must be able to name every squad since the war and make a point of telling your fellow CTs that you witnessed x event (even if you weren't actually born)

7) **Make your voice heard**

It is your moral obligation as a CT to make sure your voice is heard. On matchdays this involves sitting in a group with the other CTs and constructing loud chants that don't actually scan or rhyme. Don't worry they don't have to be witty, amusing or intelligent. Just loud.

In addition to making your voice heard on matchdays, you MUST turn up to every AGM, EGM and members forum hosted by your county. Make sure you use this opportunity to launch yourself into a rambling tirade of banal inane grumbling about how things aren't as good as they used to be and that players don't know they're born these days.

If you stick to these 7 easy steps, you can call yourself a true County Tragic. I believe you can even get a certificate.

By Lizzy Ammon

Women & Willow

The England Women's Cricket Team have been at the height of their powers over the last two years, winning the 2009 World Cup, T20 World Cup as well as holding the Ashes. They are, in fact, the product of the most sustained investment in women's cricket ever seen. England's women players no longer have to hold down jobs while attempting to train and play for their country. The world has changed.

Who could have imagined this shiny new world even ten years ago? England Women's domination of the world stage is entirely the result of the revolution that occurred when the Women's Cricket Association was brought into the ECB and sponsorship deals made for the men's team were extended to include the women's set-up. With investment at grassroots level for girls' cricket at its highest ever level too, there is now a clear path for any girl with an interest in cricket at six to progress to the national team by sixteen.

In the seventies and eighties when I was at school, the idea that cricket would be on offer to girls was unconscionable, unless you happened to be privately educated or, better yet, privately educated as one of a handful of girls in a boys' school. Instead, at the age of 14, I was told very clearly that I would not be playing cricket at school, because: "cricket is for boys".

Without any other obvious routes to playing after that particular rejection, I was 30 before I pulled on a white shirt and walked out to bat. After a couple of years playing in Oxford, I arrived in Bath, landing on the doorstep of Lansdown Cricket Club. And it is here in the friendlies and competitions of club cricket that the age and opportunity divide emerges. When I first started playing, I met a lot of women who were ten, twenty and even thirty years older , who had been playing cricket their entire lives, mostly in the clubs of London and the South East that grew and remained strong throughout the 20th century. I even played some matches against women in divided skirts. On one occasion, at an England Women's international at Bristol, I met some women in their eighties and nineties who were pioneers of the modern women's game. But equally, as the profile of the women's game has been raised by investment and sponsorship in recent years, I meet increasing numbers of women of my age and older who are new enthusiasts for the game.

The winners though, are the girls for whom cricket has been a fact of life throughout their schooling, from Kwik Cricket to Inter-Cricket and beyond. Girls who have been educated in the last ten years, now live in a world where boys and girls play cricket together from primary school age. These are the girls who discover their talent early and then find many pathways available to them by which to progress to club, county and national level.

While other clubs have worked hard to exploit new funding in

121

order to develop opportunities for girls, our team is unusual. We now have more and more young girls playing at our club but we started somewhere very different. The women's team at Lansdown emerged from a degree of boredom amongst the wives, girlfriends and mothers of the regular players. Women who figured that if they were going to spend their lives hanging about at a cricket club, they might as well make effective use of their time.

In the last two seasons, our numbers have continued to grow. Our youngest member is a talented yet occasionally crotchety fourteen year old; our oldest player is a middle-order bat, close to fifty and still a determined and successful team member with an infectious joy for her own and other's success.

We play friendlies because so many of our players have families and so cannot commit to weekly league matches and the considerable travelling in our area. We are lucky to have a handful of teams close by who share our unusual demographic, so we are evenly matched.

Sometimes, we hand out a one-sided pasting. One such occasion took place a couple of seasons ago. On a warm midsummer afternoon, our opposition's captain was celebrating her 60th birthday and we batted first, setting a very defendable score. Our opponents arrived at the crease and immediately began an excruciating collapse at the hands of our opening quick. As captain, I made a decision to ease off the gas and put a couple of our less experienced bowlers on for a few overs. The batters responded with a few runs and got themselves back on an even keel. Knowing that we needed to seal the victory after this rather generous act, I brought back our opening quick who decided, in an equally charitable gesture, to come in off a couple of paces and tweak it a little bit. The other team still felt they had a chance, and we knew we would keep down the runs. No one could have foreseen the next two deliveries, both of which clattered into the stumps from the ball gripping and turning off the pitch.

The last batsman arrived at the crease, the birthday captain, who turned to our bowler and politely suggested that she shouldn't take her wicket. The field tensed, the bowler came up to the crease and delivered an innocuous looking ball. The captain took a swipe and the ball disturbed the furniture: Game Over.

Victory on a hat-trick from the bowler. Birthday Captain looked up towards the bowler and hurled her bat onto the pitch, bellowing with some ferocity: "Arseholes!" Any notions of a genteel women's game went out of the window in that moment. It was fleeting, it was hilarious.

Occasionally we branch out to play a new side. It is on these days that we are reminded of our age and the fragility of our skills, as eight-foot-tall fifteen year olds come pounding into the crease to bowl balls of such velocity that even the most competent of our batsmen come undone, and the deliveries of our best bowlers are despatched with such vim it would cause you to cry into your cider. This is the new generation; young girls built like Amazons who have honed their skills since they were seven and are flexible enough to dive for the ball that whips toward the boundary. They look at us with disdain as though we are an alien race of women, unlike anything they have ever known. Women who know and love their own flaws, but derive a peculiar joy in trying to outwit them. Women who, let's face it, are old enough to be their mothers.

It is the club that has adjusted most, perhaps assuming that the 'ladies' would not last more than a couple of seasons. But there we are throughout every season, training twice a week and, when we have use of the home pitch, entertaining with the tightest games where moments of high drama and individual achievement are commonplace.

We are there, involved in the life of the club, taking up the largest tables at the annual Awards Dinner, making our presence abundantly felt. Some of us are more disreputable than others and at our club, our fatal flaws are quickly exposed by the Mendip Magic on tap in the clubhouse. It is the Mendip which has led some of the women's squad to find themselves standing on the bar with the men's first XI, singing songs with inexplicable lyrics.

We're not young, we're not destined for great things and we're not going to win any leagues.

But we sure do love our game.

Lucy Sweetman is still really cross with the head of PE who told her, aged 14, that cricket was for boys. Lucy didn't pull her finger out and start playing until she was 30. She is captain of Lansdown CC Ladies XI and has been playing for the club since 2004.

In Praise of...Pakistan

When the Pakistan cricket team left Heathrow after nearly three months touring England the collective sigh of relief from the English cricket community must have come close to getting their plane airborne, if not all the way back to Lahore. ECB officials, journalists and players all expressed their relief in different ways, but the basic sentiment of all concerned was summed up by more than one fan on Twitter: "Fuck off and don't come back."

Such a reaction was understandable. From the moment the News of the World revelations hit during the Lord's Test, any cricket became a sideshow, overshadowed by spot-fixing, suspensions, ball-tampering, physical violence and the ridiculous pronouncements of the Pakistani High Commissioner, Wajid Shamsul Hasan, and the President of the Pakistan Cricket Board, Ijaz Butt.
However, it overlooks one crucial fact; the cricket that took place was spell-binding.

Not all of it was brilliant; while some of the bowling was as good as anything that has been seen on these shores this century, some of the batting and fielding was captivating only because it was so spectacularly, jaw-droppingly atrocious that it offered the chance to see an international cricketer replicate the shot you played to get dismissed by your seven year old sister.

The result of this style of play was wickets, and plenty of them. Wickets are what cricket is all about – they draw the greatest cheers from the crowd and they have the biggest impact on the match. In the six Test matches that Pakistan played last summer, a wicket fell every 7.4 overs. Every 44 balls, just over every half an hour, spectators cheered as the stumps flew, the batsman edged behind or the umpire raised his finger to uphold an LBW appeal. In comparison, in the Sri Lanka v India series that went on at around the same time, it took 14.3 overs, almost twice as long, for a wicket to fall. It's difficult to imagine many spectators choosing the Sri Lankan fare over what Pakistan were serving up in England.

The wickets brought with them unpredictability. Man for man, both England and Australia were far stronger than Pakistan. Yet the ability of Pakistan's bowlers to bowl either side out in a session meant that Pakistan could never be completely ruled out, and indeed, they often emerged victorious. Of the five series they played, only the T20's against England – played in the immediate aftermath of the spot fixing revelations – were a walkover. Pakistan registered victories in every other series. Their unpredictability, and the ability to win a match from nowhere, is another part of what makes them a joy to watch.

Sadly putting Pakistan and unpredictability in the same sentence sets off metaphorical alarms and sirens screaming out 'spot-fixing'.

127

It could be that Pakistan's unpredictability is nothing of the sort, that the comedic fielding, inept batting and most of all, Kamran Akmal's farcical wicket-keeping, are all part of the script set out by the gambling kingpins in Mumbai or Dubai. The News of the World scoop appeared to show that some Pakistan players were prepared to play to order. From that point on, insidious doubts were planted in the minds of all spectators over the rest of the team's performances.

Were the simple slip catches dropped, the abject fumbles and the missed run outs simply typical examples of Pakistan's dreadful fielding, or something more sinister? Was the insipid batting in the Edgbaston test match, or the Twenty 20s in Cardiff and even parts of the ODI's in London in which they were victorious, due to England's excellent bowling, or because that's what the batsmen were paid to do? Could the record-breaking Trott/Broad partnership be believed? Fixing in any form is a cancer that undermines all the achievements, and all of the magnificent cricket that we saw last summer and before. We need a game that we can believe in.

Despite the allegations, I am sure that we would see a similar approach to the game from Pakistan even if it were guaranteed that they were clean. Earlier this summer, I saw a group of Pakistanis playing cricket in a park in Brussels, of all places. They were of no more than moderate ability, but they played cricket in identical fashion to their international compatriots. They bowled as fast as they could (which, with their elastic limbs, was pretty fast), they tried to smash the ball as far as it would go, they dropped plenty of catches, and didn't come close to picking up a ball cleanly from the ground. It's simply the Pakistan way, and the international players continue to play in the same manner they grew up on the streets of Lahore or Karachi – and it is pure box office.

Everything about Pakistan cricket screams entertainment – the players, the fans, even the administration, which matches the farcical ineptitude of some of the team's fielding. In an age where most teams believe in consistency of selection, Pakistan have used 36 players in international cricket in 2010, more than any other country. 7 of those players have been suspended or banned (4 by the Pakistan board and 3, following the spot-fixing allegations, by the ICC). 2 of those 7 played Test matches despite those bans.

It is difficult to imagine any non-Pakistani cricketers missing international matches due to genital warts – somehow it was not at all surprising for Shoaib Akthar to do just that. The supporters also mirror the team – quiet when Pakistan are struggling, passionate and raucous when they are successful. It might have upset the England team to come against a Karachi-style crowd in London, but there's no denying that the cheering, dancing, baying crowds added a sense of occasion to games that at the time were lacking anything of the sort.

Despite the ramshackle nature of Pakistan cricket, they continue to produce results. Without, even by his standards, a freak innings from Mike Hussey, they would once again have reached the final of the T20 World Cup, on top of drawing a Test series against Australia. The depth of talent in the country is vast, with no discernible change in their performance despite the constant carousel of players.

Above all, they're fun to watch, even when they're at their worst, and when they're at their best, with their fans roaring them on, there are few finer sights in cricket.

The epitome of this was Umar Gul's mastery of the old ball under the lights in the London ODI's. His beautifully controlled yorkers and slower balls sent the stumps of England's middle and lower order cart-wheeling, ignited the team and the dormant supporters, and won two games from nowhere. It was the finest, most dramatic limited overs cricket seen here since the 1999 World Cup.

There is no doubt that match-fixing must be stamped out, by the ICC rather than the PCB, but there is no reason to suspend the team or any individual players until evidence of wrong-doing emerges. Until that time, let us celebrate Pakistan, and hope to see them back in England soon.

By Stuart Millson

Fast Bowlers Don't Eat Ice Cream – Why Amir Did It

Sana Kazmi explains a young man's innocent logic behind the Lord's spot-fixing scandal...

Amir was training hard before the must-win Test at The Oval. He put in extra time in the nets with Waqar, to get closer to the stumps for his inswinger (and with Aaqib, to get closer to the optimum frequency of hair bounce per delivery). He couldn't wait to call the girl as soon as he got on the team bus. But he got distracted: Pakistan's new keeper wanted to take pictures, and nobody else was in the mood to humour him, so Amir felt bad and obliged him with enough poses to keep him busy for the bus ride back to the hotel.

When he finally got to his room and pulled out his phone, there were 25 missed calls from her, and this final text message:

"You have no balls. Don't call me again. P.S. My brother says you're 24."

92 ignored phone calls, 24 spurned texts and 18 unread emails later, he gave in and used the team's getaway identity of choice: Asif's cook, Sheeda. She didn't recognize Sheeda's Pakistan number, but still hung up when she heard Amir say hey. He was

crushed – but he hadn't been with the team long enough to surrender without a fight. He went to his big brother in the team, Salman, for advice.

"You've come to the right guy. After all, I'm the first smooth-talking Pakistan captain in ages. Even all the English journalists are saying it. The most urbane cricketer since Imran Khan..."
Cue commotion in the bathroom, where Asif was taking a leak. He stumbled out, stifled smirk on face, but when he saw Salman in his sleeveless Pakistan jersey, poking at the flab under which he always complained his biceps were hiding, Asif's muffled guffaws broke into hysterical laughter.

Salman raised a single luscious, aristocratic eyebrow.

"Sorry, man. Every time someone compares a player to Imran *Bhai*, this happens. It's just one of the nasty side-effects of my vitamin supplements."

"You mean those goat-milk extra-strength pills your village doc gave you, that make you pee every 21 minutes, and especially after your spells end?"

Luckily, Salman was a gentleman (read: not Shoaib), so no bats were raised and Asif emerged from the bathroom with his own words of advice on relationships. Citing his tremendous experience in the matter, Asif told Amir that it was ridiculous to waste his tears on a girl who didn't read her email.

"Dude, my ex would even check *my* email!"

He urged Amir to get his fix of intricate beauty from bowling instead and launched into a tireless lecture setting batsmen up. All Amir could make of it was "mindfuck" and "KP", so he went back to sulking with his unresponsive phone. Salman saw the need for leadership and seized the opportunity:

"Why don't you tell me what really happened in the nets today?"

"She's crazy. She was watching us practise with her friends and wanted to show off every delivery I've got."

"Well, that's kind of cute."

"Anyway, I told her there wasn't time because Wiqi *Bhai* was only supervising one over per bowler, and I only had 2 balls left. She got on my case to bowl no-balls! To prolong my spell!"

(Asif snorted a laugh but was immediately shut up by another raised-eyebrow glare from Salman).

"No, he's right. She thought a no-ball would mean an extra ball. In the nets! And she won't let me explain – what am I supposed to do!"

"Look, it's just a couple of no-balls. Let's just have you bowl them in the match. As a gift for her. Pick a meaningful number, like, your anniversary and bowl your promised delivery of love in that over. It's genius!"

"Anniversary? I met her 2 weeks ago, with you, at that ice-cream parlour opening you dragged us to."

"Oh, right, this is the girl who's a steward at Lord's..."

"Hasn't discovered email, doesn't give a fuck about cricket yet works for one of its most esteemed institutions. Reminds me of Uncle," Asif chimed in.

"Asif, you're testing my patience again. Ijaz Butt is **not** related to me. Anyway, ignore him, kiddo. So, how many times?"

"Well, this would've been our third date, but our first *special* one."

"Let's make it the first ball of the third over, then? I'll write it down in my strategy notebook too, so we won't forget. By the way, you guys should really read these notes sometime. Did you know the English media calls me an Anglophile?"

"Uh-huh."

"Anyway, this plan is golden. You will literally bowl her over – ha! See what I did?"

"I guess it's worth a shot."

And so it was. Amir crossed his fingers and thumbed a text to the girl to deliver this promise of enduring love. Unfortunately for him and Pakistan, Mazhar Majeed joined the boys in Butt's room soon after the plan was finalised. He sneaked a look at Butt's open notebook, which gave him all the information he needed for a perfect spot-fix, as long as he got to make the call on which ball in which over would demonstrate his 'influence' (a task made easier by the compliant News of the World staff who showed no interest in picking the timing themselves).

However, holding up his promise would prove to be a handful for Majeed.

He had not anticipated that Asif would proceed to share stories of his ups and downs with the ladies. Somewhere between the village vamp who spiked his lassi with HGH and the B-grade Lollywood actress who framed him in the theft of her red-hot

Ferrari (a tale that never failed to elicit a curious yelp from Yasir Hameed), Amir started to question whether a girlfriend was even a good idea. Besides, every night after dinner, Shoaib Malik emailed the team a YouTube clip from the extensive media trial Asif's ex put him through.

"It was brutal, like bowling to Sehwag on a Faisalabad road," Asif admitted.

This was starting to make Amir want to flee, all the way back to the border-town near the Taliban-infested Swat Valley where Geoff Lawson thought he grew up. He was so scarred by the tales of Asif's trials, you would think he had developed antibodies against women: he didn't bowl a single no-ball in what ended up being a match-winning spell at the Oval.

Majeed had failed to deliver on his promise to NOTW and it was time for him to be proactive. He had to ensure Amir delivered the no-goods come Lord's. It took some key strategy documents from the top-ranked side and a Bank Holiday weekend special of high school rom-coms like Clueless, but he finally managed to convince this 18-year-old that girlfriends were good.

Or so he thought. The night before the day of the planned no-ball, Amir texted him:

"Shall I do it or not..?"

Majeed almost had a nervous breakdown, but there was little he could do except warn NOTW it might not happen.

Amir didn't hear from Majeed but it didn't matter. He told himself this was it: this was going to be his day. He could feel it. And so could anybody watching. He bowled with fire and heart, and had four wickets before anybody knew it was time for his third full over.

Except *he* knew it. He wasn't nervous, but he wanted to make sure he got it right. He turned to Salman one last time. The long discussion that followed had many keen observers of the game guessing (and one Pakistani in South London throwing his white BlackBerry at his TV).

"This is it, Salman *Bhai*. This is the right decision, right?"

After one final review of the positive externalities of loving for fast bowling, Amir walked back to his mark. He bowled that no-ball. The girl was at the ground. She smiled, he sensed it, and everyone watching saw it all in his bowling – relief, freedom, love. That *sajda* after the 5-fer was not just for God and cricket. Rob Smyth was right: It was not a kiss of betrayal, it was the kiss of a boy who loved his cricket. And his girl.

Sana Kazmi is a reformed (read failed) computer scientist and a wannabe social entrepreneur. She tweets, mostly about cricket, at twitter.com/sanakazmi

137

20 Inconvenient Truths Suppressed by the Global Media Conspiracy

Cricket has a well-earned reputation for generating the finest sporting prose. Over the years it has seduced multi-talented writers like Pinter, Beckett, and CLR James. The best writers on cricket today are still the few remaining pluralists like Gideon Haigh, for whom cricket is a passion, and not a monomania.

However, lately, devotees have been served up a bland *smörgåsbord* of arse-licking commentators and uninspired reporters, for whom the most searing insight is derived from the twitter feeds of young men trying to find a synonymous phrase for "hey bru, congrats on your hundred. C U 'N [Cape] Town :P ha ha" [sic, sic, sic...].

The result is a furious and frustrated public that authorities hope will eventually be lobotomized into slack-jawed dribbling drones, gawping at the profundity of yet another cricketer as he explains how pleased he is with his form in the nets. That way no soul will bat an eyelid when they scrap Test cricket altogether, and charge us £80 for a five-over thrash spread across two hours of live performance advertising.

Therefore, since we seem to inhabit the media equivalent of late East Germany, I shall take this opportunity to say 20 of the things that consenting adults may utter in underground bars, but if heard by the ICC would result in 30 year banning orders from cricket grounds worldwide...

1. Don Bradman was an unspeakable tosser who actually averaged only 56.37 (if you discount all the matches when it was decreed bowlers had to bowl a full length outside off-stump to give him a chance). He was a mean-spirited career destroyer who cast aspersions on bowlers' actions if they dared to get him out. Especially if that bowler happened to be a native Australian. If I was making a movie, he'd be played by Charles Laughton with Matt Damon as Douglas Jardine, and Brad Pitt as Harold Larwood.

2. Giles Clarke sold English cricket to Allen Stanford. Either he knew Stanford was a crook or he's just a greedy buffoon who cannot organise due diligence. Mohammed Amir may or may not have sold the fourth ball of *that* over for a few thousand pounds. Giles Clarke is still in his job. Mohammed Amir is suspended. Go figure.

3. All post-match interviews with players are carefully orchestrated propaganda that serve only to destroy our brains. We should lobby for players to be administered truth serum, so instead of Ricky Ponting shiftily assuring us that Nathan Hauritz is bowling fine, he can say: "Aww, look here mate, have you seen the rest of our spinners? Sure Nathan is diabolical shit, but the cupboard

is bare. And I really miss Warnie even though he bags my captaincy. Why does everyone hate me by the way?"

4. Umpires don't deserve respect, they earn it. It's not so hard a job standing around in a perpetual summer, scrounging free meals, orthopaedic double mattresses in five-star hotels and obligatory late-night porn. Some of them are good. Some of them are mediocre. And Billy Bowden is an unbearable self-publicist who gives incompetence a good name. And don't give me any shit about arthritis – I've seen him straighten that finger.

5. Did I mention that Giles Clarke is still in his job?

6. Andrew Flintoff is not a national treasure. He's a tax exile at a time of crippling financial crisis. And his stats were only good for two years. The rest of the time he was a hopelessly unfit talent-waster who got by on his big grin and matey hugs. He should be stripped of his UK passport and made to spend the rest of his life in a slowly shrinking cupboard with just James Corden for company until they get wedged together like the couple representing Lust in Se7en.

7. Dickie Bird was a terrible umpire.

8. Tony Greig's exorbitantly priced, Channel 9 sponsored memorabilia has no sell-on value.

9. After Billy Bowden, Indian fan banners are the most annoying things in the world. "India, please do well today", "MS Dhoni, we think U R very good", "Take sum [sic] wickets Bhaji, and then we wil [sic] win". The

perpetrators of these outrages are a disgrace to a proud nation.

10. If you skip a Test to attend the birth of your baby, you raise the interests of the individual above the needs of the collective. Mr. Spock in Star Trek wouldn't stand for it and neither do I. If you do the same to attend the wedding of your sister, you're a total wuss and should be banned from playing for at least three years.

11. All *doosras* are pretty illegal. It's not racist to say this. When Hauritz bowled a doosra on the last day of the 2nd test between India and Australia, it was a bona fide chuck. When Saeed Ajmal does it, it is also a chuck. Umpires should call a no-ball if an off-spinner turns the ball from leg to off. End of story.

12. Shane Watson is actually a pretty good cricketer.

13. The people who bother to respond to live polls during IPL matches involving questions as idiotic as "do you think King's XI Punjab have a better batting side than a bowling side" should have their calls traced and immediately carted off for corrective cognitive therapy. I reckon you'd clean up most of the anodyne Indian banner writers into the bargain (see point 9).

14. Ian Botham's pitch reports are always wrong. Take his advice, invert it, and bet accordingly. You will become rich.

15. When David 'Bumble' Lloyd loses the power of speech at the sight of an attractive woman in the crowd, it's

creepy. It's hardly his fault. He's old and has a turkey's neck. But it sure is creepy.

16. Ian Bishop has never said a profound or insightful thing, in his entire life.

17. Michael Vaughan's much acclaimed captaincy in the 2005 Ashes series was atrocious. Sure, he got Hayden out to a tricksy short mid-off once or twice, but his failure to bowl Simon Jones at both Edgbaston and Old Trafford nearly cost England the Ashes. He makes Ponting look like Brearley.

18. Danny Morrison, Laxman Sivaramakrishnan and Ravi Shastri are the three worst people at their jobs in the known universe. Are they blackmailing someone? How else have they not been put on trial for 'Crimes Against Accurately Describing What The Hell Is Going On Out There'?

19. Viv Richards uses the word "individual" way too much on the few occasions they let him commentate.

20. Bill Lawry was never out LBW in Australia because for years, Australian umpires cheated.

I'm now changing my name to Robert Maxwell and heading off to St. John's Wood for a chinwag with that marvellous chap at the ECB. Is it still Giles Clarke?

By Daniel Norcross

Eight Players to Watch in 2011

Adrian Barath, **20 [WI]** – For a young man of short stature, Barath packs an incredible punch with the bat. He announced himself on the international scene with 104 in his debut Test at Brisbane, in an innings where the next highest score was just 26. Brian Lara had caught sight of Barath in the nets when he was just 11, and there is more than a hint of Lara in his own batting, with a hyper-extravagant flick of the wrist when playing on the leg-side.

Barath has put in some whirlwind performances for Trinidad & Tobago at domestic level as well as in the Champions League T20, and he has the talent to take the World Cup and IPL by storm this year. Barath and Gayle could well become the most exciting opening partnership in world cricket.

Callum Ferguson, **26 [AUS]** – Ferguson's career has twice been stalled at crucial junctures by serious knee injuries – once on the eve of the U19 World Cup, and then in the Champions League T20 Final. Despite this, he continues to pile on the runs as a tremendously improved player at state level in the past two years.

Ferguson has taken to international cricket like a duck to water, proving himself to be the man for a crisis with his superb temperament. His skills were best seen in T20 cricket, where he has been exceptional for South Australia with his clean striking while finishing off an innings. He seems to have an excellent cricket brain in terms of knowing where to find the gaps in the field, and has a calm head on his shoulders – you don't often see him get out to irresponsible shots. If given the chance, he will be a star of the World Cup.

Ferguson has yet to say anything remotely arrogant in his career to date, leading neutrals to question whether he really is Australian. He will be a star of the World Cup.

Jimmy Adams, 30 **[ENG]** – A few years ago, Adams was a fringe county player, captaining the 2nd XI and getting odd games for the main Hampshire side. Now he is one of the best openers in the country over all formats, second only to the great Trescothick in my view.

Whether it be the morning of the first day of four or the start of a limited overs innings, Adams brings his no-nonsense, conscientious 'A game' every time, and bats with conviction. What has been even more remarkable is his transformation within a transformation. The 2009 season saw Adams become a mainstay of the four-day team followed by a spot in the limited overs sides mid-season. 2010 was the season during which he truly announced himself as a versatile opener, blitzing the T20 and its run-scoring records. In addition, his sublime fielding makes him a key figure throughout an entire match.

To watch Adams is not to watch a whirlwind whiz make waves en route to international stardom. It is more an appreciation. An appreciation of the sort of cricketer who makes the game what it truly is. A vital, efficient cog and a fantastic batsman to boot.

Adams is the only player in our list with no international recognition to date, but if he keeps up his form then it is surely only a matter of time, perhaps after the inevitable English World Cup purge?

Darren Sammy, 27 [WI] – The first ever cricketer from St Lucia to play internationals, Sammy truly is a marvellous cricketer. He plays with tremendous heart, always diving around the field and setting the standard for his lethargic team. Given his team credentials, it was a refreshing step forward for the notoriously myopic WICB to appoint the inexperienced but enthusiastic Sammy as captain of the national side.

He's not the best batsman, he's not the best bowler, and his tactical astuteness while leading a team of lazy wantaways remains to be proven. However, he will no doubt try his utmost, and it could be one of the great cricketing success stories if he does well at the World Cup. Assuming he is drafted, Sammy could prove to be one of the value buys of the IPL.

Sammy not only makes our team for his boundless enthusiasm,

but also for his bizarre tweeting, with strange and cryptic messages during his honeymoon with his new wife.

At first, we were unsure as to whether Sammy was posting in-jokes or whether he was delirious from undergoing one of the most traumatic experiences in a man's life, and so we gave him the benefit of the doubt. However, it soon became strange. Almost so strange that it could not be true. All of his followers were wondering the same thing – was Darren Sammy really tweeting the world about his sex life?

Sammy's strange metaphor-cum-fantasies always revolve around his 'Queen Bee' and 'honey from the comb'.

For example:

"1month to date…ants still following my marriage trails…cause the honey overflowing…taking wifey to dinner..
then..hmm…sweet as…

Looking forward to spending quality time with my Queen B and enjoy the honey she produced..

Waking is so easy when u know the person next to u is sexilicious…sweet as..then I'm mentally prepared to play around fine leg region…"

We started off by pretending to have misheard the man, giving him the benefit of doubt – personally, I naturally assumed that his wife was a master beekeeper of some sort, and was famed for her honey-producing skills. Of course, with a master beekeeper for a wife, it was only natural for Sammy to be proclaiming his love for her wonderfully sweet honey.

But this is the straw that broke the camel's back:

"My balls will be swinging in and out today and I'll get the break thru the gully region...but also my fineleg will be closely monitored"

If our worst fears are true, the man really needs to come up with some new, more cryptic metaphors which his followers can then take to be digs at the opposition fielding or the WICB...not non-too-subtle hints about how he always raises his bat and points to his wife in the crowd whenever he's on 69 not out.

An anecdote about Shivnarine Chanderpaul getting into a fight with Marlon Samuels over who cooks the best jerk chicken is an example of the gossip we love to hear about. Even proclaiming your love for your new wife is par for the course on Twitter. But short of openly admitting that he and his wife engage in animalistic caveman sex from dawn til dusk every single day, Sammy really keeps giving us a bit more than we'd bargained for. Tone it down for 2011, please.

Angelo Mathews, 23 [SRI] – Imagine Stuart Broad a few shades darker, intelligent, and at the absolutely opposite end of the humility spectrum, and you end up with somebody resembling Angelo Mathews.

Mathews has somehow managed to usurp Farveez Maharoof as Sri Lanka's premier all-rounder, despite essentially being exactly the same player. The only notable difference is that Mathews has managed to start putting in some match-winning performances with both bat and ball, and he can become a fulcrum for Sri Lankan cricket in years to come. His death bowling needs improving but with experience, he could become one of the best around. Sri Lanka's World Cup hopes rest on Mathews, and he has the temperament to deliver.

Cheteshwar Pujara, 22 [IND] – After stroking a match-winning fourth innings knock on debut versus Australia, the world finally found out what a select few had been saying for years – that Pujara is going to be the next great Indian batsman. Boldly promoted to number 3 after a first-innings failure, the young man from Gujarat played one of the all-time memorable debut knocks with a glorious 72.

An unhappy Kolkata Knight Riders side was not a great place to mature such a prodigious, orthodox talent, and as such, his development may well have been impaired by having such shitty players around him, but Pujara has gone a long way to proving

148

himself after just one glorious innings. His flicks of the wrist are reminiscent of Laxman, but with a more compact technique Pujara can perhaps become an even more versatile player. It is also noteworthy that he is one of relatively few batsmen to have made his debut in a Test match in recent times, with most being given the opportunity to prove they can slog in the ODI death overs first.

Pujara has a tremendous future ahead of him, and there is little doubt that he is the most talented young batsman in the world right now.

Steve Smith, 21 [AUS] – Even though Steve Smith looks like a mutant extra in The Hills Have Eyes, he is actually not too bad a cricketer. In fact, Smith has the makings of a fantastic batsman, so it's rather bizarre that he has been fast-tracked into the national side as a raw leg-spinner who will get pounded from pillar to post, at which point he will inevitably decide that leg-spin is really a great big waste of his time, and just end up concentrating on his batting.

The fact that Smith has been plunged into the national side at such a young age is indicative of Australia's desperation for the next Warne. We accept Smith's ascension heartily, as the world is desperate for an Australian all-rounder who might relieve us of that malignant tumour of cricket, Shane Watson.

Smith will inevitably be mismanaged in 2011. He really is a poor spinner – as a first-class average of 50 testifies – so forcing him into bowling 20 over spells in Sri Lanka will probably be counter-productive. However, Smith is a bloody good batsman in the shorter forms of the game. He should get a decent IPL contract and his career path is already reminiscent of Cameron White at an early age. Similarly, expect Smith to soon give up the tricky art of leg-spin after some chastening experiences in the IPL and World Cup.

Virat Kohli, **22 [IND]** – Kohli might as well go around wearing a giant condom on his head, because he is by far the biggest dickhead in world cricket. In a world where we already have to contend with Watson, Haddin, half of the South African team, Kevin Pietersen, Harbhajan…did I mention Watson? Considering we are living in an unrivalled era of dickishness, Kohli's achievement is all the more impressive.

For the past few years, Kohli was termed a 'precocious talent'. Sadly, he got caught up in his own hype, and proceeded to do extremely dickish things like put in a ridiculous earring stud and walk around with an undeserved strut. In spite of this, Kohli is a talented cricketer who managed to secure a permanent ODI slot for the foreseeable future with some impressive knocks in during 2010, and he certainly has the ability to do well in the World Cup on lifeless home surfaces.

A universal schadenfreude highlight of 2010 was during an IPL match (yes, really), where Kohli was coming close to pulling off an improbable chase for Royal Challengers Bangalore, virtually single-handedly. When he was unable to hit a last-ball boundary, Kohli sunk to his knees a lá Brett Lee/Edgbaston, struggling to take in the emotions of being unable to secure victory for a team nobody supports, in a league which nobody cares about.

His partner Rahul Dravid felt compelled to come over and console young Kohli, before realising that he'd inadvertently been trapped into a cunning photo-op. Even the most die-hard England fan felt some sympathy for Brett Lee, but we couldn't help but laugh in Kohli's face.

To quote @eyepeeell on Twitter:

"Virat Kohli's mother put powdered Viagra in his milk. No other explanation for why he's grown up to be such a big dick."

by Nishant Joshi & Half-Tracker

Cheatsheet – How to Write a Cricket Diary

I assume you are an international or first-class cricketer and you've come here looking for tips on how to write your diary. I've put together a cheatsheet for you. In it is all the basics you will need to make sure that book is so formulaic that no sponsors will leave you.

Employ a ghostwriter. Pick a writer who is not that famous but who is skilled as a ghostwriter. You obviously won't want to sit down and write, that is for angry talentless people, so you need a ghostwriter. Find one who thinks you are great, and then sit down with him for two days. From there, the book writes itself.

Teammates. All your teammates are great. Some might be out of form, but they train hard and will come back. Some might be in trouble with the law, but that donkey they fucked clearly consented before the group sex, and the boys obviously thought it was male. You can never put enough praise on them; after all, they are the greatest bunch of blokes you have played with, every single one of them. Use their nicknames as well; make us feel like part of the team.

The media. They don't really understand you. Even though your writer is part of the media, and you are talking to him now, you hate them all. They say you live in a bubble, but *they* do. They make things up, blow things out of proportion and end the career of hard working, hard living cricketers. Question their sexuality as well.

Your Hotel. All fans of yours will really want to know every detail of your hotel.

Ex–cricketers. The problem with ex-cricketers is that they forget about the pressure. You should really drill this home. Once a guy leaves cricket he will start to bag you, so bag the fucker back. If he says you are shit, question his record, or personal life. All ex-players turn evil (by joining the media), so abusing them is OK.

Your family. Even if your wife and children are annoying fuckers, you must say you miss them at least thrice on every tour. Also put in some details about how much your kids have grown/changed etc. and how your wife is such a terrific wife.

Famous people. If, during the period of the diary or near enough, you met someone famous in another field, include that, and then say really nice, but meaningless, things about meeting them. Then get them to write a boring, meaningless foreword as well.

Charity work. Even if the only charity you believe in is fucking the odd ugly fan, you cannot release a book about yourself without mentioning some charity work. The best charities should be about cricket and or cancer. If you can't come up with one, I always thought a cricket testicular cancer charity called 'One Short' could work.

Apologia. Think of the book as your chance to explain all of your actions. No one can interject or use logic to stop you, your book is one long explanation for everything you have done wrong – well, that others think you've done wrong.

Opposition players. If there is an opposition player that pisses you off, don't get snippy with them in a press conference, do it in your book. If you are particularly angry, it means free publicity. **Praise the fans**. This may surprise you, but most people in cricket don't like you, so use your book to suck up to the fans. Start each chapter with, "the fans at (enter place name here) are some of the most passionate and informed fans in cricket.

Your name. You are famous; your name will sell shit. Put it large on the cover, and ignore the ghostwriter. He is no one, you are a cricketer.

By Jarrod Kimber

The Alternative XI 2011

Our prestigious team has been selected by our esteemed panel of writers, and showcases the best of cricket as it was meant to be – handlebar moustaches, dreadlocks and beer.

You don't need to have scored the most runs in the calendar year and you don't even have to be a particularly good player – we simply want to acknowledge those who continue to fascinate and entertain. This is our appreciation of the under-appreciated.

Our selections are not picked so that we need to choose some token players in order to placate fans of every nation…so apologies to Australian, Sri Lankan and Bangladeshi fans. Maybe if your players are more inclined to become involved in orgies and match-fixing in the coming year, then we will be able to open up some spots.

Jesse Ryder (NZ) – A mercurial batsman who has played a handful of powerful innings, our Jesse is 25 years old and has already battled alcoholism. A tragedy for sure, if it weren't so fucking hilarious.

The thing about Jesse is that being an idiot, he celebrates 100 days of abstinence by going on an all-night bender. After a successful series with the bat, he punches a window (perhaps he caught sight of his own reflection), abuses hospital staff, and is out for months.

Such stupidity can only be applauded.

We love the bloke – ballsy batsman, overweight, and drinks like there's no tomorrow. He is cricket's very own Paul Gascoigne, and should be treasured as such.

However, I am sure we all have a common fear; that it is only a matter of time before Jesse pisses into a jar full of Don Bradman's remains and proclaims himself to be the greatest batsman of all time, whilst dancing precariously on top of the Lord's media centre. Already looking into a career after an inevitably early retirement, we are reliably informed that Jesse is being groomed to be a spokesman for the Darwin Awards.

Chris Gayle (WI) – Imagine: you're on The Titanic. You've been hit by an iceberg, and while you're trying to 'accidentally on purpose' lose your nagging wife, a dreadlocked giant of a black man saunters his way past the house band in a sharp tuxedo and sunglasses.

Amidst all the panic, this one man smirks momentarily as everybody stares at him. The house band cease to play 'Nearer, my God, to Thee', as if on command from a higher power.

The ship falls silent, and people even forego seats on lifeboats in order to stay on deck and witness what might happen next.

Gayle stares back at the crowd, quizzically, as if to say: "Why you stop dah party, man?" He moves his lips apart ever so slightly, and his teeth gleam magnificently as he allows himself a modest smile.

Then, he suddenly fades into the darkness, drawing gasps. He quickly re-emerges, whipping out an emergency steel drum kit. He always knew it would come in handy.

He ponders asking if there are any requests, before brushing his lapels and belting out 'No Woman, No Cry' on drums. Showcasing the full extent of his miraculously white smile, he rocks back and forth in a half-reggae, half-samba fashion. His dreadlocks wave effortlessly from side to side.

The Titanic descends into the depths, and as you start to gasp in freezing sea water, your pain is numbed by the sound of a nonplussed Jamaican singing along to 'One Love'.

Chris Gayle scored his second Test triple century in 2010, joining an elite group of only four players to have reached the landmark twice. This is the same man who was stripped of the national captaincy for basically not wanting to play Test cricket. Gayle would be captain of The Alternative XI, but we don't want to be seen to be picking up leftovers – after all, we're not the ICL.

VVS Laxman [IND] – I tell you what, if you're a batsman in a shit run of form, just undo all of your shirt buttons. All of them.

Don't be embarrassed; unless you're Ian Bell and your chest hair endowment consists of a single tuft of pubic-looking hair, in which case feel free to conceal your inadequacies.

Laxmans' ample chest hair, gold chain and classic technique all hark back to a time when batsmen just batted and bowlers just bowled. As cricket fans, we all live in Laxman's world. His leftover crumbs of *roti* should be served as ambrosia to us mere mortals. In stricter interpretations of Laxmanism, posturing that the great man is even capable of spilling crumbs can be seen as blasphemy.

After all, he is the only member of the Indian side who turned up to Sreesanth's spaghetti night and left with a white shirt perfectly intact. The fact that he passed on all of Sree's appetite-killing 'Spaghetti Curry Surprise' to Yuvraj is besides the point.

It is often said that some of the great Indian batsmen verge on 'demi-God' status, but Laxman is the only one who could well turn out to be incarnate of a divine being and we wouldn't be surprised.

Laxman's second innings rearguard actions have been a path to enlightenment for all who have witnessed his genius in such situations. 2010 was a perfect example of his abilities. He is certainly the greatest exponent of batting with the tail in the modern era, and perhaps he will be recognised as the best of all

158

time in this respect.

In 2010 alone, he managed to save a Test against New Zealand with his team 15/5 in the third innings; he scored a match-winning fourth innings century on a crumbling pitch in Colombo, and he stroked a scarcely believable 73* against Australia in a one-wicket win at Mohali.

His calmness defies all logic and convention. There was never a sense of panic. Moreover, he instils calm in his lesser talented tail, who are then inspired to bat with application and determination. Laxman is a shepherd and hapless tail-enders are his flock.

Two of those innings were completed with Laxman struggling badly with back spasms, underlining that he is a player who is only able to express himself fully when he is in the toughest situations possible. Even if he was bound with a straitjacket, Laxman would still find a way to pirouette his way to victory.

Laxman remains the most attractive man in the Indian side, despite having the appearance of a pharmacist in 1970's Mumbai.

Jonathon Trott [ENG] – If there was a nuclear holocaust tomorrow, it would not surprise you to see Trott as the sole survivor. His cockroach antennae would now be visible, but you would still recognise him from his occasional outbursts of Tourette's, in a distinctly bastardized South African-English hybrid accent.

The shame about Trott is that despite being a well-respected member of his own team, opposition players seem to get incredibly wound up by him. In the 2009 Ashes, Trott was sledged for his 'time-wasting' idiosyncrasies at the crease, where the Aussies managed to make a deal out of him 'digging a trench' inside his own crease. What else would you expect from someone who treats every innings like the Battle of the Somme, an unyielding war of attrition in which the the dirt below soaks up his sweat and blood. And he loves it.

Trott has played a handful of backs-to-the-wall innings for England, but his finest moment surely came in the summer of 2010, when he apparently managed to get into an altercation with Wahab 'The Jacket' Riaz, after allegedly riling him about being implicated in the spot-fixing scandal.

However, instead of coming to blows like real men, the two sissies had to be separated after Trott allegedly struck The Jacket with his batting pad. I'm hardly a mixed martial arts expert myself, but perhaps Trott needs to realise that striking a grown man with a piece of foam is not going to cause any long-lasting damage. There are unconfirmed rumours that a deranged Trott subsequently walked around like a pimp, shouting "HOW YOU LIKE ME NOW, BITCH?!" to a confused Wahab.

Hashim Amla [SA] – In ODI's in 2010, Amla scored 1,015 runs @ 75.6, with five centuries and four fifties in just 15 innings. That he scored his runs at a strike rate of 104 makes his form even more remarkable, for Amla was often criticised for being a placid player, who could potentially make a decent Test batsman but would be too conservative for ODI's. Lest we forget, this is a man who played 22 Tests before he was given a chance in the ODI arena. Curiously, being given an opportunity in ODI's has clearly loosened any shackles which once bound Amla, and as a consequence his all-round game has improved tremendously in the past three years, culminating in 2010 as his *annus mirabilis*. An uncluttered mind and a state of pure Zen have transformed Hashim Amla from a player of style sans substance, into a player of substance with style.

Now, he is South Africa's undisputed MVP, which is no mean feat in a line-up with Smith, Kallis and de Villiers. Among neutrals, he is now also South Africa's most popular player, which in fairness, is an altogether easier task.

It's tempting to compare Amla's 2010 to Mohammad Yousuf's record-breaking 2006 – both players are wonderfully still and calm at the crease, with an artist's backlift and wrists that an ambidextrous masturbator would be proud of. Both exhibit unparalleled tranquility, a wonderful serenity at the batting crease, and we are blessed that Amla can play with such grace and style on testing home pitches.

They also have the biggest beards since W.G Grace, but I'm sure you already drew the comparison as soon as I mentioned their names.

Scott Styris [NZL] – For a man whose face must have been a scientific experiment to form a hybrid between a pig and an ass, Styris has done remarkably well for himself. A journeyman cricketer with no special skills to speak of, he was picked for New Zealand after 10 years of toiling on the domestic circuit.

Styris has managed to impress sporadically throughout his international career, rarely putting in match-winning performances but always contributing in classic New Zealand fashion – under-appreciated and bordering nondescript. As the latest reincarnation of Chris Harris, Styris is a classic 'dibbly-dobbler' as he trundles into bowl. He could be one of the few bowlers on the international circuit who should forego a run-up altogether, as the ball seems to come out of his hand slower than his jog to the crease.

Shahid Afridi [PAK, CAPTAIN] – A shoe-in for the Alternative XI, Afridi's life is so chaotic that he has become an embodiment of everything to do with Pakistan cricket – a huge imbalance between talent and intelligence.

His smooth, silky run-up is always a joy to watch with his equally silky hair bouncing along. As per usual, Afridi had plenty of moments in 2010, most of them involving some form of controversy.

His year began with an incident in which he literally tried to eat a cricket ball, and was given a two-match ODI ban. A few days in a padded cell would have not gone amiss. He also managed to fit in a reintroduction into the Test side as captain, before hastily retiring from Tests after just two matches back in the fold.

Afridi the cricketer had a pretty tepid year, with modest returns with the ball (19 wickets in 18 matches @ 45.0) and improved, if inconsistent performances with the bat (601 runs @ 33.3), begging the question as to who is so stupid as to continue selecting this man for international cricket, when it is quite clear to all that he is a brainless slogger with the bat, and when there are also better spin options. Crowds flock to stadiums in Asia to see 'Boom Boom' but I wouldn't waste my hard-earned money on coming in just to see someone who might well knock me unconscious with a six and then get out next ball. Afridi's form has always been fleeting, so any innings lasting longer than 20 balls should be treated with shock.

There has simply got to be something going wrong in Afridi's head. Few have had more international knocks than him, and he cannot give any excuses for top-edging an attempted slog every single innings.

There are so many wonderful quotes that have come out of Afridi's mouth in the past year, it's tough to know where to start, but just two will suffice:

"It could have been a police case because it is a crime to hit someone. But we showed a big heart and did not press for it." – Afridi on the Trott/Wahab incident. Really, Shahid? You showed 'a big heart' by not prosecuting somebody for patting your player with a styrofoam pad? With this attitude, we can only assume that Afridi pats himself on the back every time he flushes the toilet.

In response to an undercover interview with Yasir Hameed by the News of the World, Afridi said that Hameed 'has a mental age of 15'. When somebody who once ate a ball calls you immature, you know you have problems.

Overall, Afridi is the boy who you keep wanting to slap in the face for being naughty, but you can't because he keeps on playing with his penis.

Kamran Akmal [PAK, WK] – quite possibly the most universally hated player of all time, the eldest Akmal brother is a bizarre enigma. Despite being a talented batsman, Iron Gloves Akmal is clearly the worst wicket-keeper of all time. It's a shame, because Akmal might have been a good one, were he not impaired by his unique congenital deformity of having cymbals for hands.

164

After a farcical Test in Sydney '09, where Akmal managed to drop four catches and miss an easy run-out chance, Akmal has had the constant spectre of match-fixing hovering above his head, although we should stress that to date, nothing has been proven. Unlike others, there have been no photos with bookies or wire taps – our only suspicions are aroused by the question: "Can anybody possibly be that bad?"

These days, the Pakistan team don't celebrate taking wickets; they celebrate Akmal holding onto a catch.

The Akmal brothers all have faces only a mother could love, but one can only assume that in this case, their mother is visually impaired, or like the rest of us, she is repulsed at the very sight of her own offspring. Even though we chose to support the AYCSO in this book, it was a tough decision to overlook the plight of the Akmals, who each suffer from a debilitating case of ugliness. At the very least, we considered sending a beautician to their house for an eyebrow threading session.

Kamran and Umar already disprove the theory that two brains are better than one, and with younger siblings chomping at the bit to get in the side, we may well end up with a team with the lowest aggregate IQ scores in sport.

There are rumours that some of the Pakistan team might end up in big trouble, as if Kamran doesn't already have the appearance of a Lahore bookie's choice gimp. If it reached the point of high treason, you could imagine the co-conspirators pushing Kamran forward to be first in the guillotine.

Moreover, if he ever ends up in jail, you would have to feel for poor Kamran. With his butterfingers, you would fear for the lad every time he gets hold of the soap in the prison showers.

Graeme Swann [ENG] – almost so Alternative that it would be subversive to leave him out. All the same, he plays the game with a smile on his face, and has helped to rejuvenate the art of off-spin, without resorting to throwing in a doosra here and there. He has become famous for trying to prove how funny he is via Twitter, which was refreshing, for the first day I suppose. As we are essentially anarchic and nobody likes a try-hard, Swann is a borderline pick, but gets the nod for his ludicrous drink-driving charge.

Caught driving above the legal limit in the middle of the night, he protested his defence by claiming that his cat was stuck underneath a floorboard, and that he was rushing to a DIY store – in the middle of the night – in order to pick up some tools. What type of society do we live in where our star cricketers are supplied with Rolls Royces but not with screwdrivers? And why did we not hear the testimony of this mysterious, scientific marvel of a cat, who can apparently morph through Italian redwood?

166

Shoaib Akhtar [PAK & desperate IPL side] – any fast bowler who makes a full thirteen comebacks and peaks at 35 years old deserves some credit. This is the same man who was shamed publically for being a walking STD clinic, by his own cricket board no less.

Shoaib serves as a walking anti-promiscuity advert to any prospective cricketer, having shown the world how genital warts can somehow put you out of the game. It's hard to understand the logistics of his affliction, unless the shaft of his penis is the source of his powers. If Shoaib was playing the role of Clarke Kent, his Kryptonite would probably be a combination of flat pitches, curfews, training, and dental dams.

The fact that he was out 'injured' due to genital warts indicates that poor Shoaib must have had a serious flare-up, exhibiting symptoms of burning, itching, and the obligatory emotional distress which seems to accompany most PCB press releases.

It is remarkable that Shoaib is still playing cricket, and not a burned-out second-hand car salesman who lives in a caravan with his Russian bride. 2010 was the ultimate renaissance for Shoaib, as he managed to regularly clock 150kph, in lethal, short bursts in ODI's. His stats of 19 wickets @ 32.0 are not going to be widely recognised, but anybody who has seen him play will have taken note of his efforts.

Particularly in light of one of the worst years of any sports team in history, it is remarkable when we realise that Shoaib has been a relative beacon of integrity compared to the rest of his pathetic team. He is one of a handful – if that – of Pakistan's players whose name has not been associated with any match-fixing rumours, and at his grand old age, we wonder whether Shoaib has become tired of controversy and has at last decided to focus solely on his bowling.

The 2011 World Cup is likely to see Shoaib's international swansong, and I am confident that if given backing from his captain and support bowlers, Shoaib could have some epic moments of catharsis.

Mohammed Amir [PAK] – Currently serving a suspension over allegations of spot-fixing, Amir really fucked us over: Amir was like the girl next door who turned out to be a filthy coke-sniffing stripper.

When the infamous News of the World story broke during the Lord's Test, there was an incredible feeling of betrayal and overriding sense of "Say it ain't so, Amir…"

We looked on helplessly as damning evidence emerged surrounding one naïve village boy's indiscretions. We didn't give a shit about Asif, Butt, or anybody else. We all wanted to believe that Amir had been forced into delivering those no-balls, as if he had a gun to his head and had no other option. We hoped the truth would emerge and he would be proven innocent, and that Asif and Butt would be condemned with life bans as if to emphasise Amir's innocence.

The sad fact about the spot-fixing incident is that it has proven how quickly you can descend into the murky depths of disreputability with just one indiscretion. For a few weeks, Amir was the hottest property in cricket as he ripped through the Australian and England line-ups on a consistent basis. He had it all – pace, swing and seam. He was unplayable, and regardless of affiliation, we openly gushed about him being the next Wasim Akram. He was the perfect combination of youth, raw talent, good looks, and blissful innocence.

If Mohammed Amir had launched his own brand of hair conditioner before the Lord's Test, I'd have bought the bottle just to marvel at his cherub face on the label. Now, I would still buy any of his hair products, because his hair still retains its awesome sheen without ever looking greasy, but I would turn the bottle the wrong way round so as to avoid becoming teary-eyed every time I was to take a shower.

If Amir ever walks past me, I will stop him and tell him how disappointed I was when I heard the bad news, but that he will always have our support because cricket fans are forgiving people.

I would then revert to being stern again, and say: "Son, your hair may be pure, but alas; your heart is not."

It would give me the perfect opportunity to take advantage of his transient re-guilt and confusion by slowly, unforgivingly running my fingers through his glorious, glorious hair.

By Nishant Joshi

Email: home@thealternativecricketalmanack.com
www.TheAlternativeCricketAlmanack.com
Twitter.com/TheAltAlmanack

260245BV00001B/26/P

9 781456 399504